You Can't Win Them All, CHARLIE BROWN

by CHARLES M. SCHULZ

Selected Cartoons from

"Ha Ha, Herman," Charlie Brown, Volume 2

FAWCETT CREST • NEW YORK

A Fawcett Crest Book
Published by Ballantine Books
 Published in the United States by Ballantine Books, a division of Random House, Inc., New York, and simultaneously in Canada by Random House of Canada Limited, Toronto.

ISBN 0-449-21580-6

This book comprises the second half of "HA HA, HERMAN," CHARLIE BROWN, and is reprinted by arrangement with Holt, Rinehart and Winston, Inc.

Manufactured in the United States of America

First Ballantine Books Edition: October 1983
Thirteenth Printing: February 1990

You Can't Win Them All, Charlie Brown

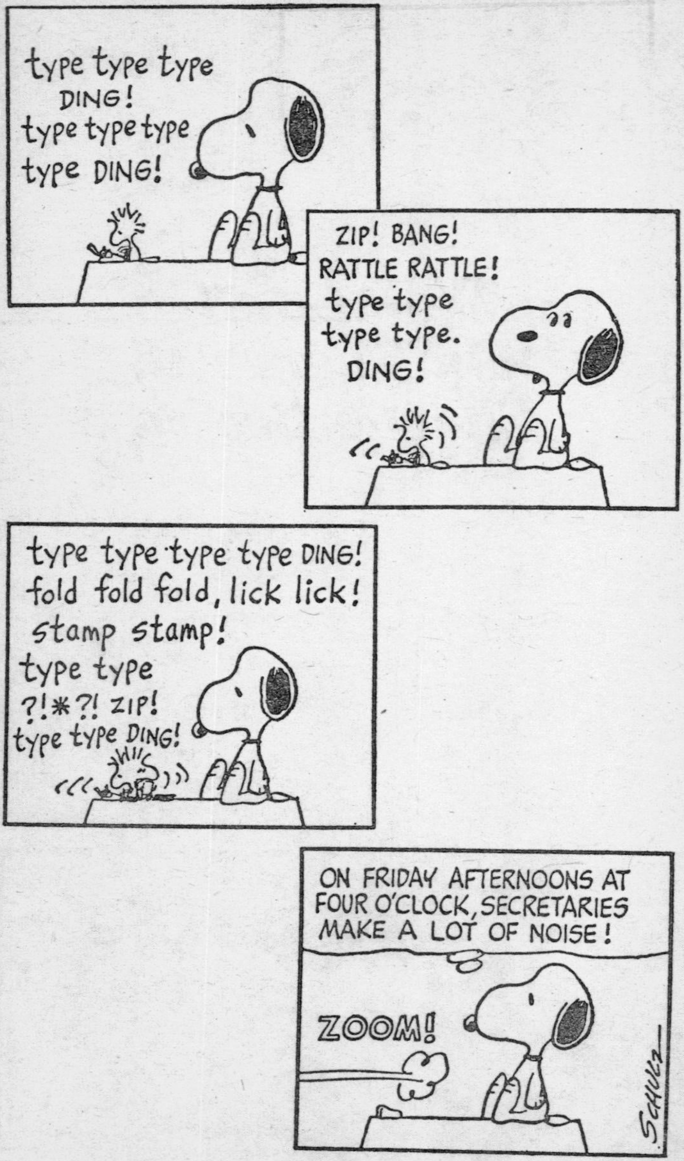
type type type
DING!
type type type
type DING!
ZIP! BANG!
RATTLE RATTLE!
type type
type type.
DING!
type type type type DING!
fold fold fold, lick lick!
stamp stamp!
type type
?!*?! ZIP!
type type DING!
ON FRIDAY AFTERNOONS AT FOUR O'CLOCK, SECRETARIES MAKE A LOT OF NOISE!
ZOOM!
SCHULZ

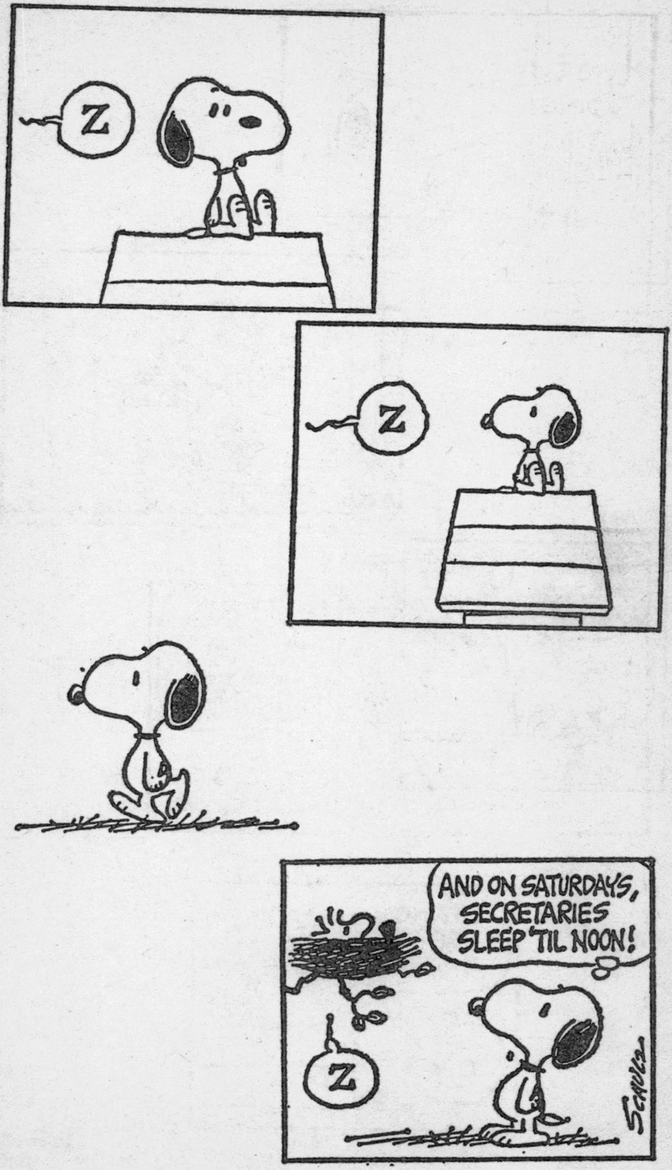
Z
Z
AND ON SATURDAYS, SECRETARIES SLEEP 'TIL NOON!
Z
SCHULZ

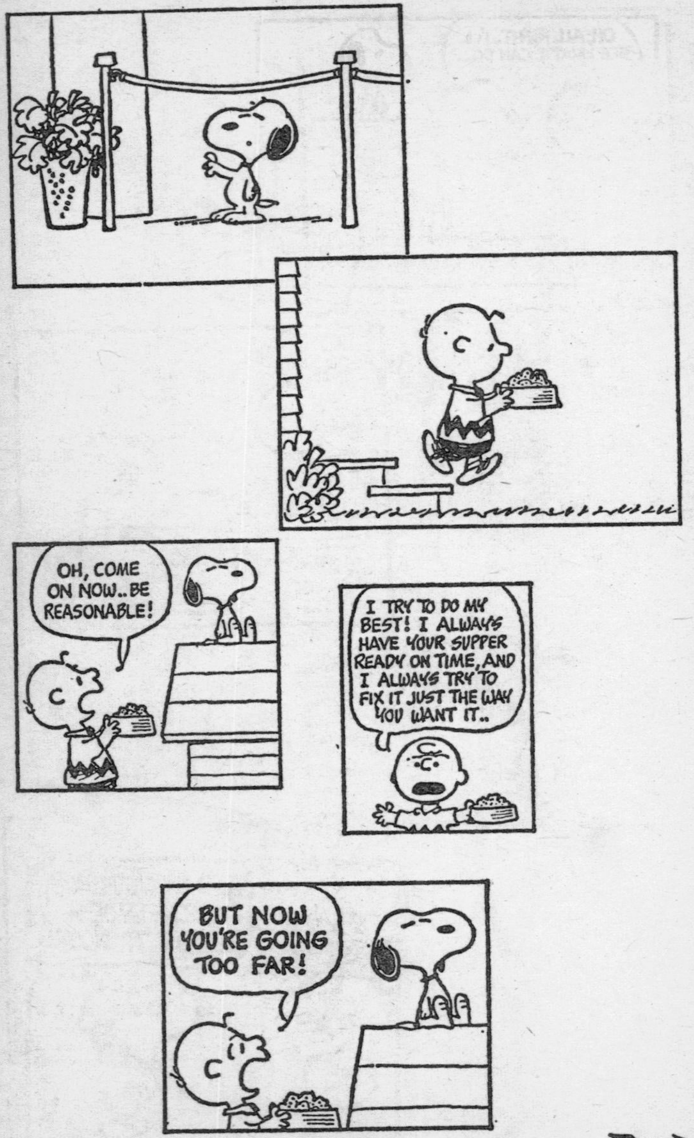
OH, COME ON NOW.. BE REASONABLE!
I TRY TO DO MY BEST! I ALWAYS HAVE YOUR SUPPER READY ON TIME, AND I ALWAYS TRY TO FIX IT JUST THE WAY YOU WANT IT..
BUT NOW YOU'RE GOING TOO FAR!

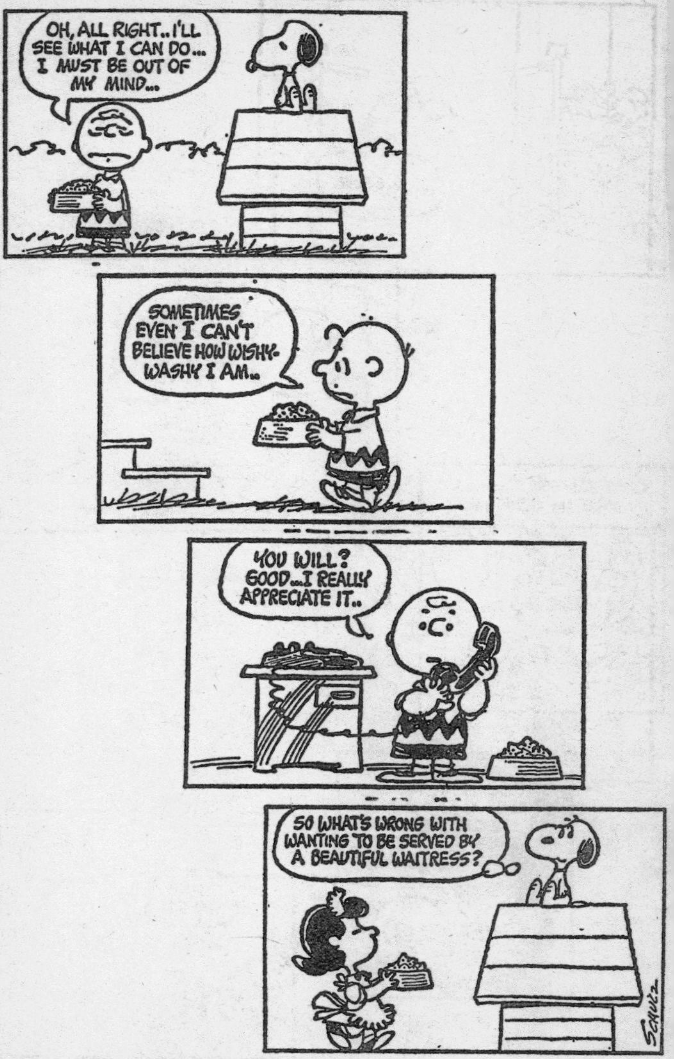
OH, ALL RIGHT.. I'LL SEE WHAT I CAN DO... I MUST BE OUT OF MY MIND...
SOMETIMES EVEN I CAN'T BELIEVE HOW WISHY-WASHY I AM..
YOU WILL? GOOD...I REALLY APPRECIATE IT..
SO WHAT'S WRONG WITH WANTING TO BE SERVED BY A BEAUTIFUL WAITRESS?
SCHULZ

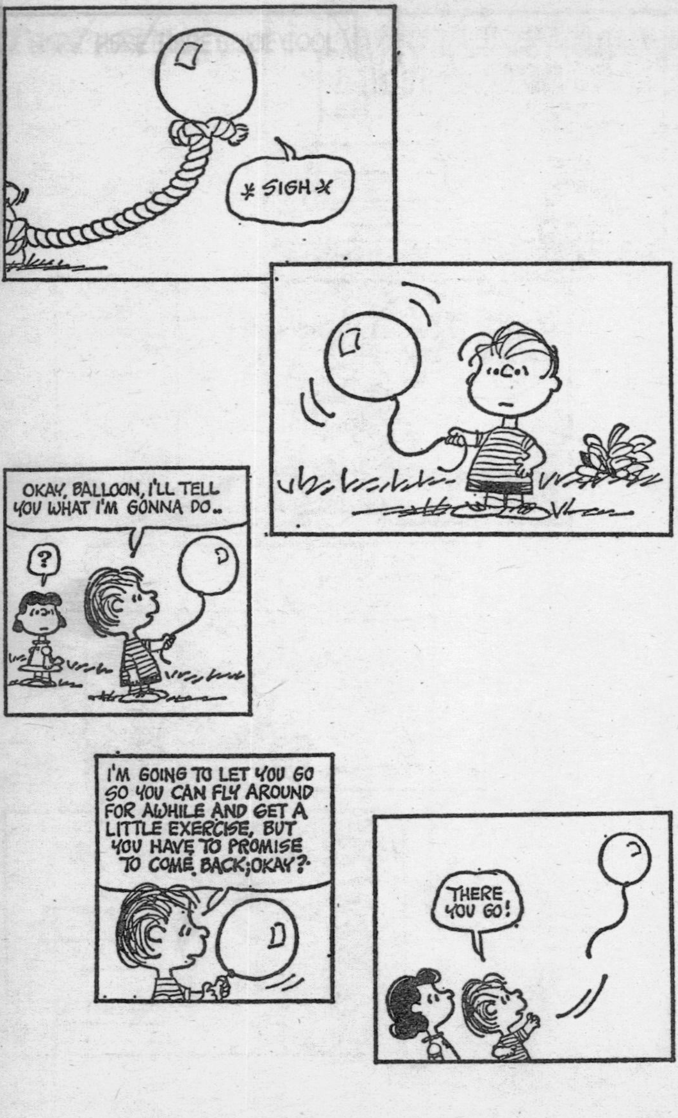
* SIGH *
OKAY, BALLOON, I'LL TELL YOU WHAT I'M GONNA DO..
?
I'M GOING TO LET YOU GO SO YOU CAN FLY AROUND FOR AWHILE AND GET A LITTLE EXERCISE, BUT YOU HAVE TO PROMISE TO COME BACK; OKAY?
THERE YOU GO!

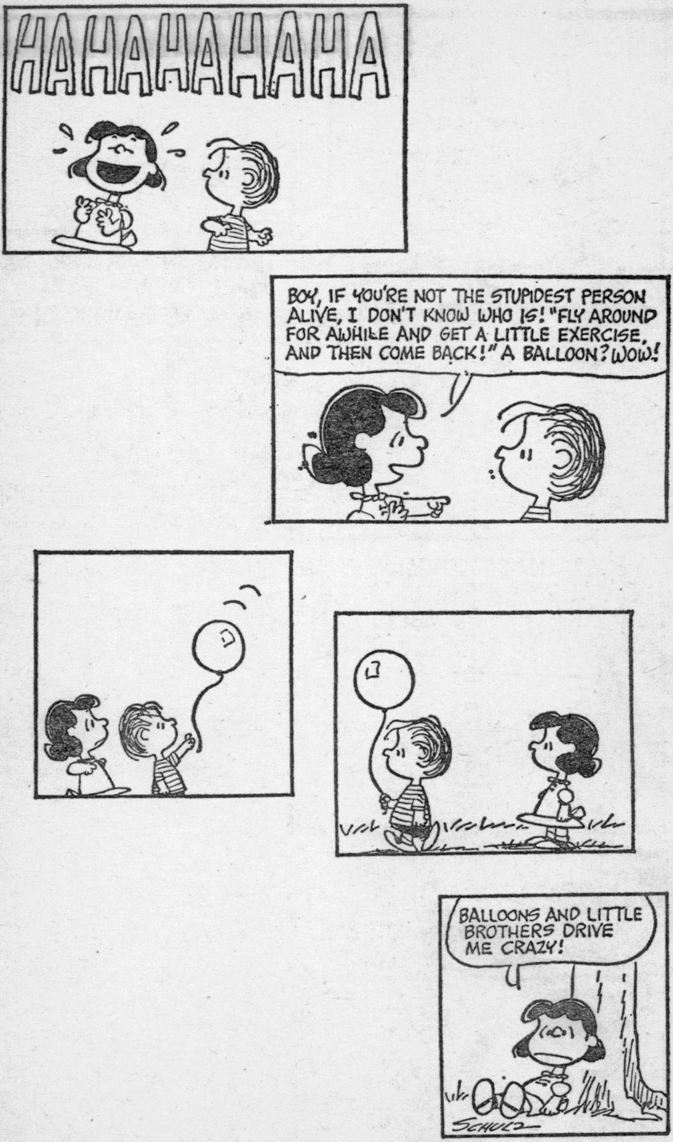
HAHAHAHAHAHA
BOY, IF YOU'RE NOT THE STUPIDEST PERSON ALIVE, I DON'T KNOW WHO IS! "FLY AROUND FOR AWHILE AND GET A LITTLE EXERCISE, AND THEN COME BACK!" A BALLOON? WOW!
BALLOONS AND LITTLE BROTHERS DRIVE ME CRAZY!
SCHULZ

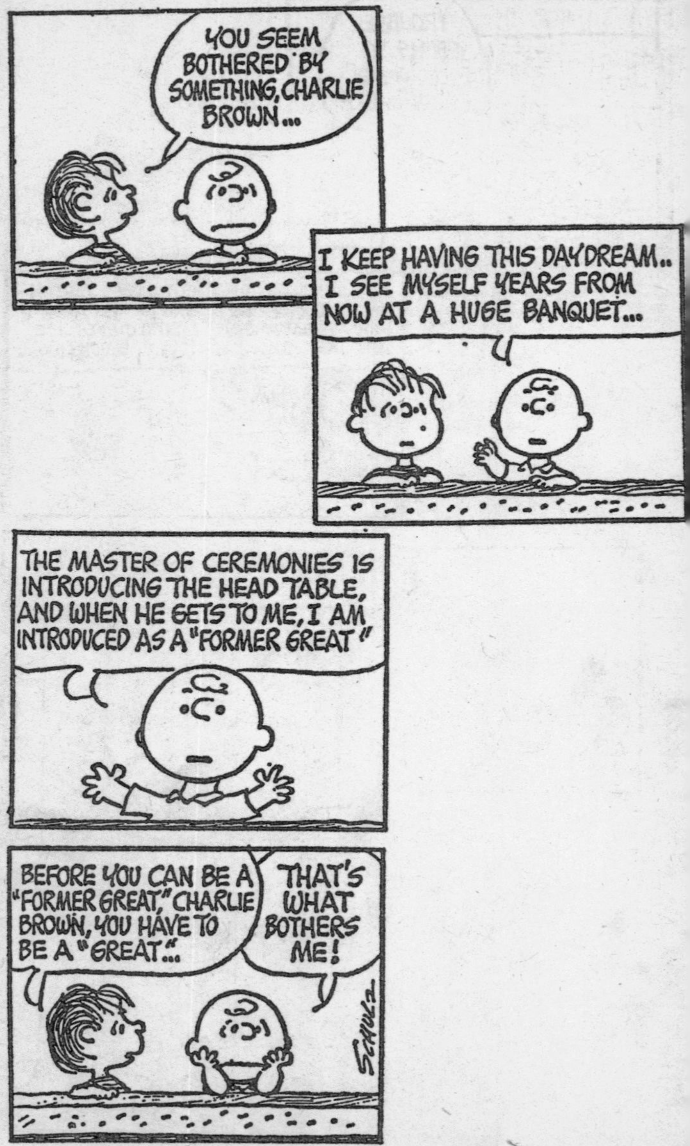
YOU SEEM BOTHERED BY SOMETHING, CHARLIE BROWN...
I KEEP HAVING THIS DAYDREAM.. I SEE MYSELF YEARS FROM NOW AT A HUGE BANQUET...
THE MASTER OF CEREMONIES IS INTRODUCING THE HEAD TABLE, AND WHEN HE GETS TO ME, I AM INTRODUCED AS A "FORMER GREAT"
BEFORE YOU CAN BE A "FORMER GREAT," CHARLIE BROWN, YOU HAVE TO BE A "GREAT"...
THAT'S WHAT BOTHERS ME!
SCHULZ

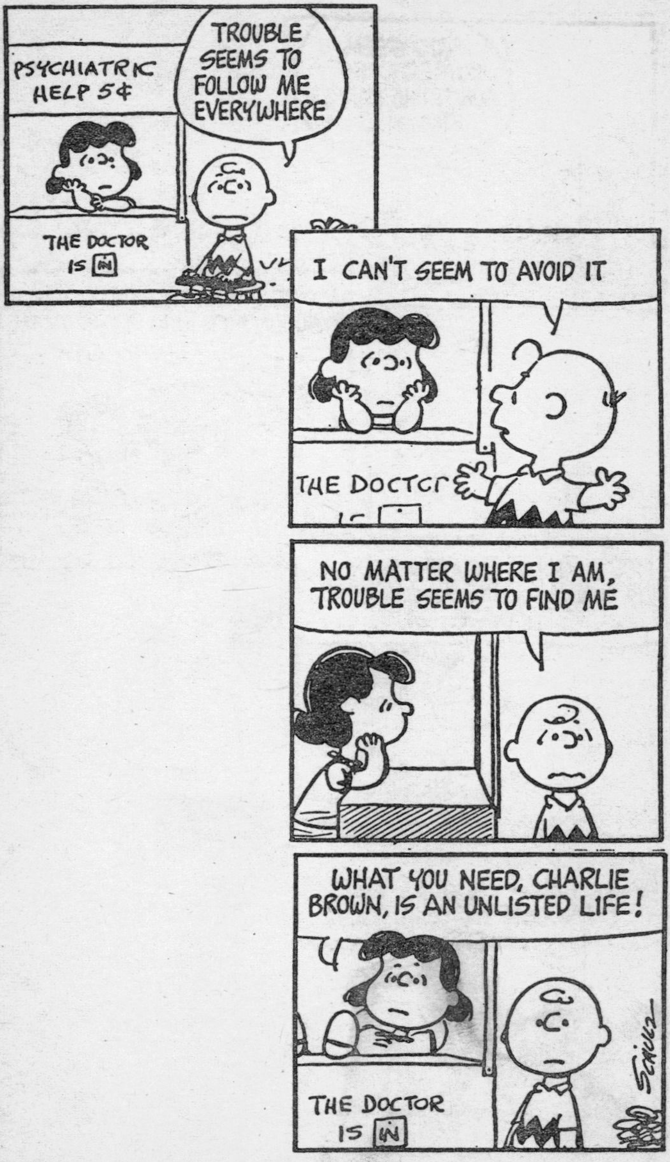
PSYCHIATRIC HELP 5¢
THE DOCTOR IS IN
TROUBLE SEEMS TO FOLLOW ME EVERYWHERE
I CAN'T SEEM TO AVOID IT
NO MATTER WHERE I AM, TROUBLE SEEMS TO FIND ME
WHAT YOU NEED, CHARLIE BROWN, IS AN UNLISTED LIFE!
THE DOCTOR IS IN
SCHULZ

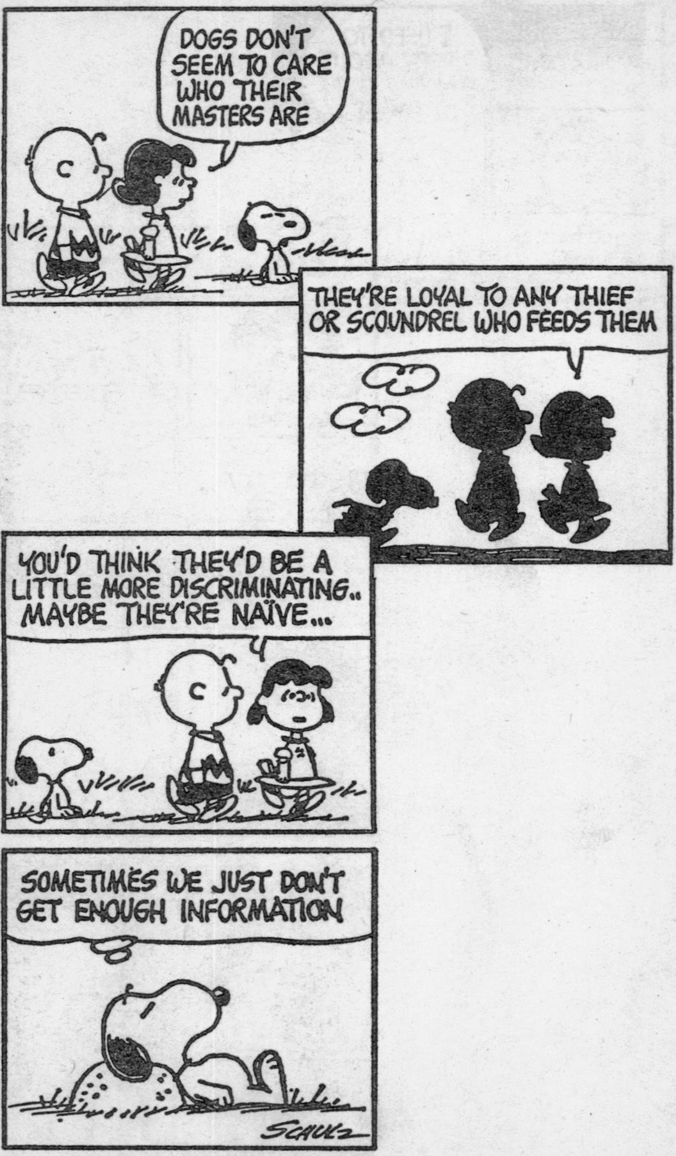

DOGS DON'T SEEM TO CARE WHO THEIR MASTERS ARE
THEY'RE LOYAL TO ANY THIEF OR SCOUNDREL WHO FEEDS THEM
YOU'D THINK THEY'D BE A LITTLE MORE DISCRIMINATING.. MAYBE THEY'RE NAÏVE...
SOMETIMES WE JUST DON'T GET ENOUGH INFORMATION
SCHULZ

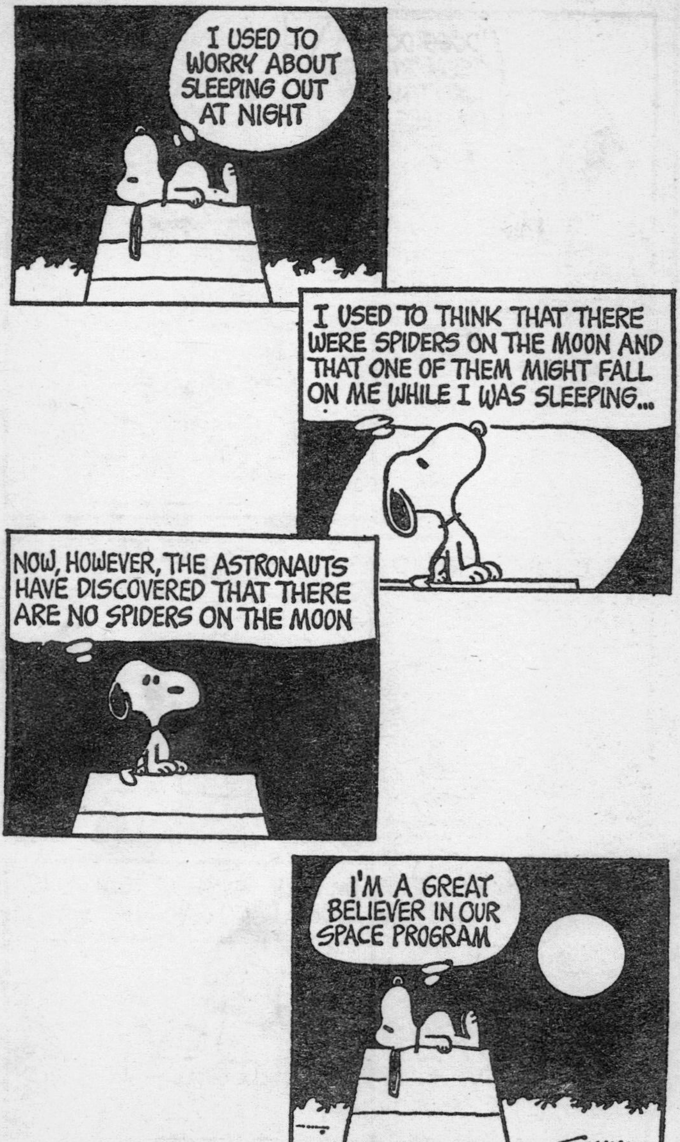

I USED TO WORRY ABOUT SLEEPING OUT AT NIGHT
I USED TO THINK THAT THERE WERE SPIDERS ON THE MOON AND THAT ONE OF THEM MIGHT FALL ON ME WHILE I WAS SLEEPING...
NOW, HOWEVER, THE ASTRONAUTS HAVE DISCOVERED THAT THERE ARE NO SPIDERS ON THE MOON
I'M A GREAT BELIEVER IN OUR SPACE PROGRAM
SCHULZ

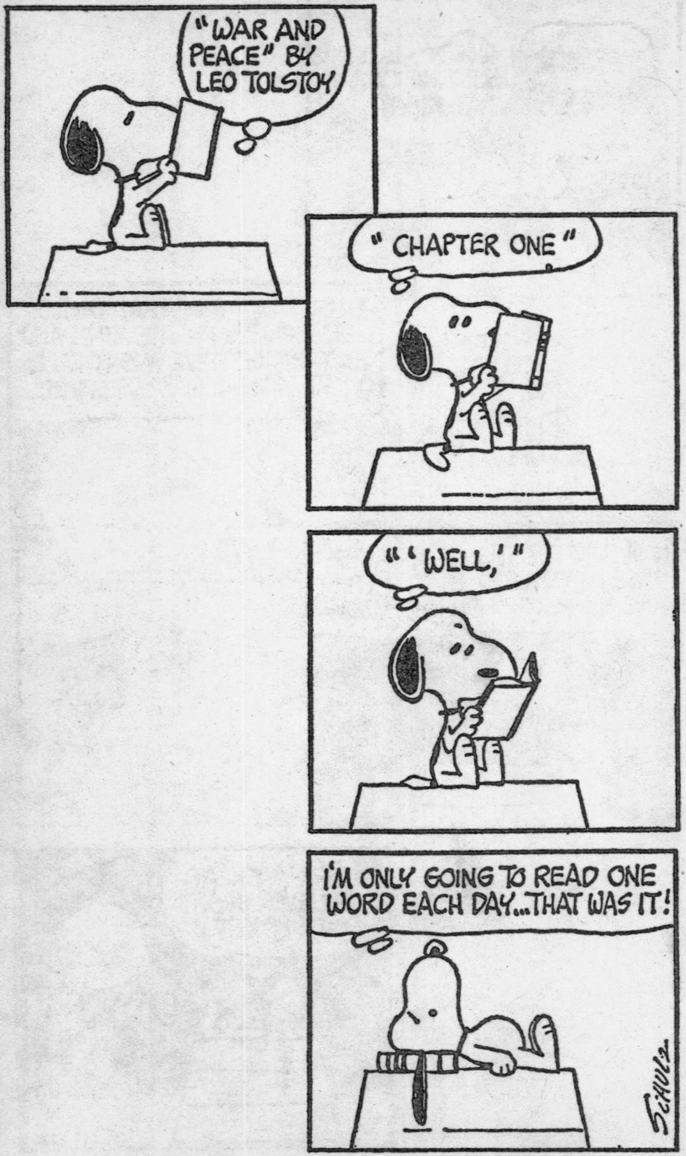
"WAR AND PEACE" BY LEO TOLSTOY
" CHAPTER ONE "
" 'WELL,' "
I'M ONLY GOING TO READ ONE WORD EACH DAY...THAT WAS IT!
SCHULZ

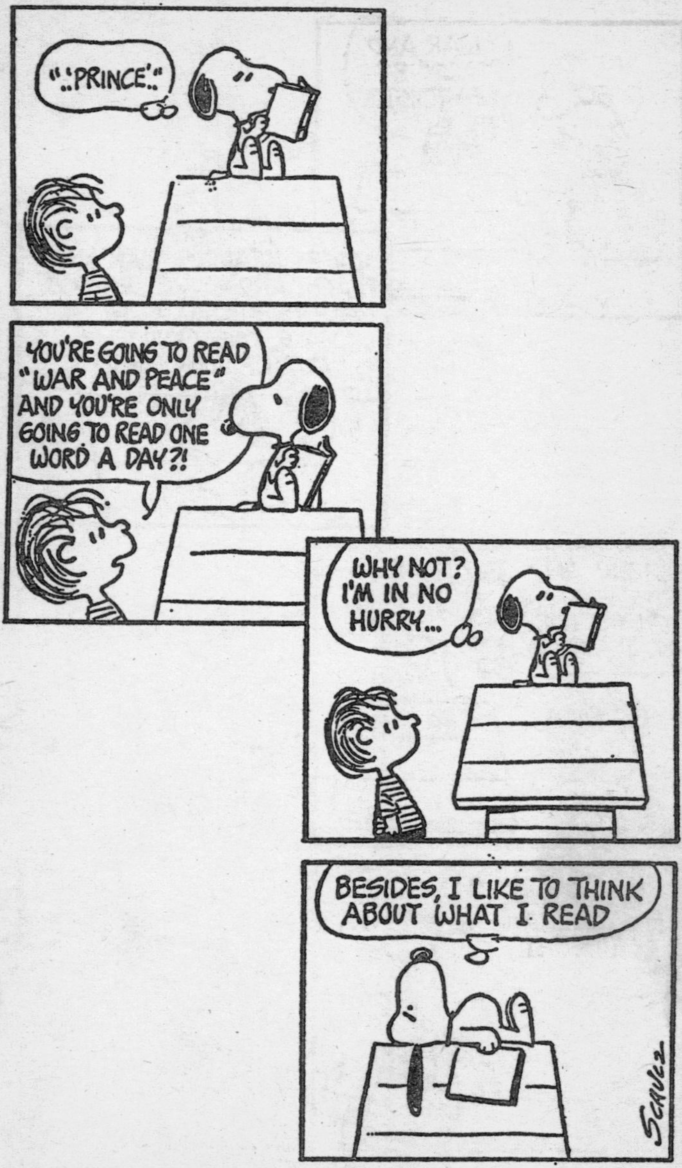

"..'PRINCE'.."
YOU'RE GOING TO READ "WAR AND PEACE" AND YOU'RE ONLY GOING TO READ ONE WORD A DAY?!
WHY NOT? I'M IN NO HURRY...
BESIDES, I LIKE TO THINK ABOUT WHAT I READ
SCHULZ

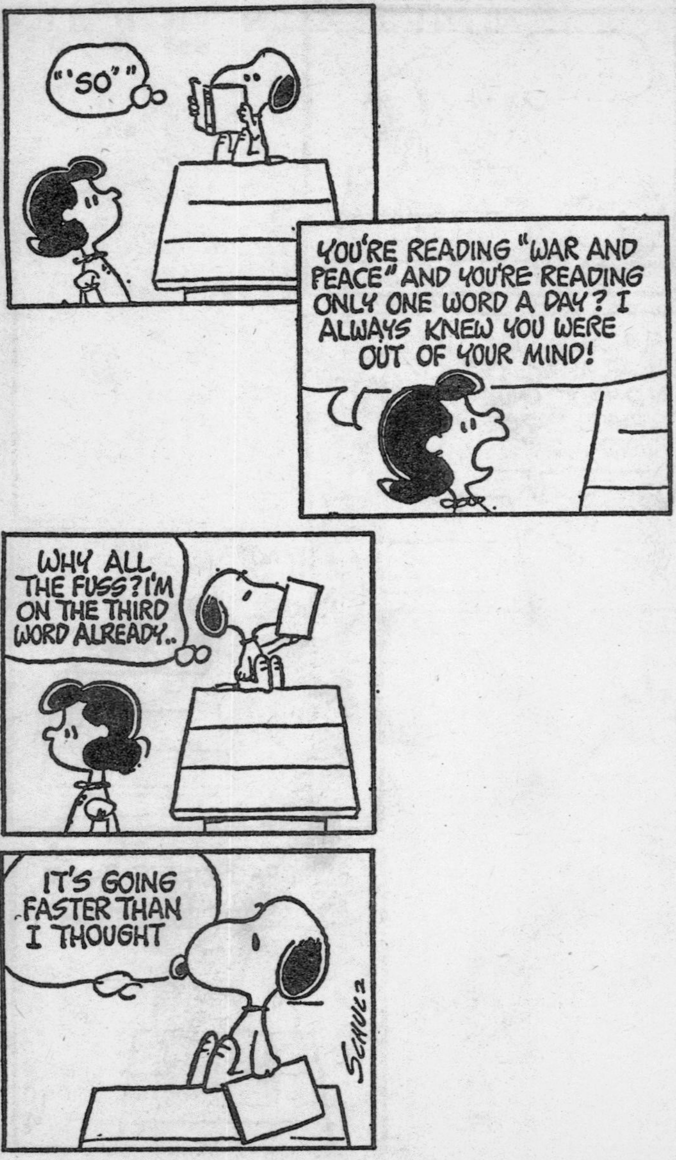
"'SO'"
YOU'RE READING "WAR AND PEACE" AND YOU'RE READING ONLY ONE WORD A DAY? I ALWAYS KNEW YOU WERE OUT OF YOUR MIND!
WHY ALL THE FUSS? I'M ON THE THIRD WORD ALREADY..
IT'S GOING FASTER THAN I THOUGHT
SCHULZ

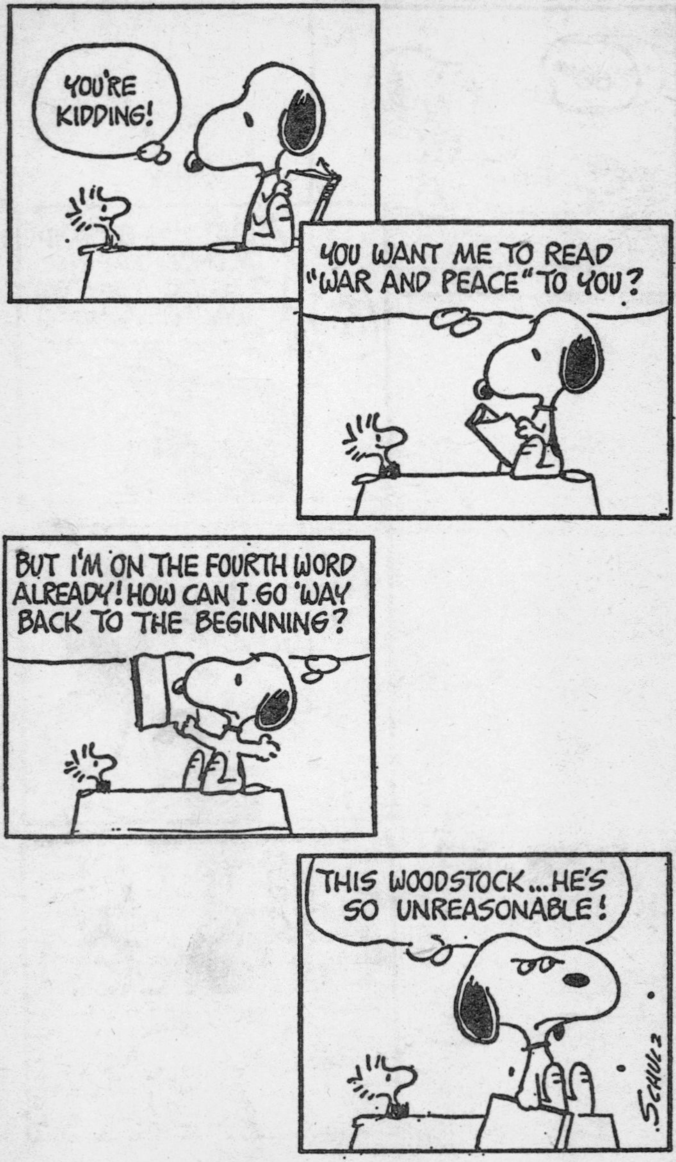
YOU'RE KIDDING!
YOU WANT ME TO READ "WAR AND PEACE" TO YOU?
BUT I'M ON THE FOURTH WORD ALREADY! HOW CAN I GO 'WAY BACK TO THE BEGINNING?
THIS WOODSTOCK...HE'S SO UNREASONABLE!
SCHULZ

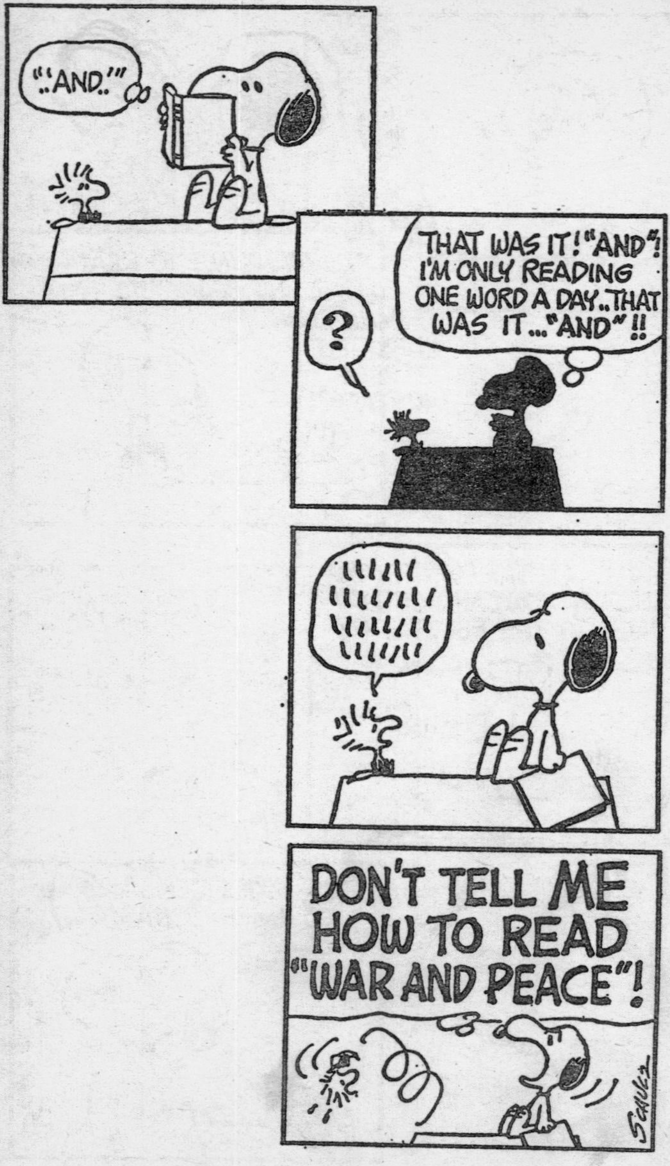
"..AND.."
THAT WAS IT! "AND"! I'M ONLY READING ONE WORD A DAY.. THAT WAS IT... "AND"!!
?
DON'T TELL ME HOW TO READ "WAR AND PEACE"!
SCHULZ

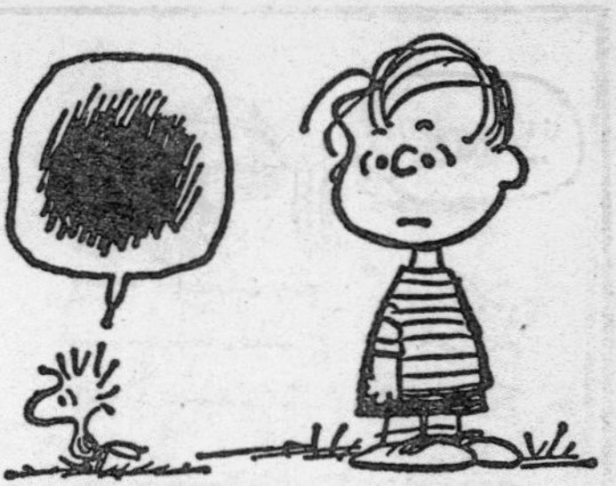

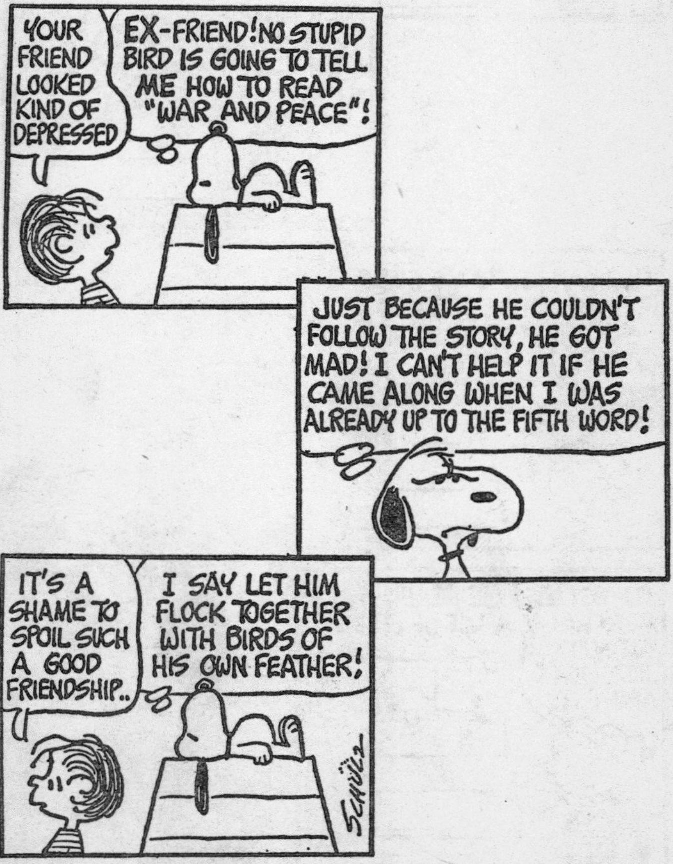
YOUR FRIEND LOOKED KIND OF DEPRESSED
EX-FRIEND! NO STUPID BIRD IS GOING TO TELL ME HOW TO READ "WAR AND PEACE"!
JUST BECAUSE HE COULDN'T FOLLOW THE STORY, HE GOT MAD! I CAN'T HELP IT IF HE CAME ALONG WHEN I WAS ALREADY UP TO THE FIFTH WORD!
IT'S A SHAME TO SPOIL SUCH A GOOD FRIENDSHIP..
I SAY LET HIM FLOCK TOGETHER WITH BIRDS OF HIS OWN FEATHER!
SCHULZ

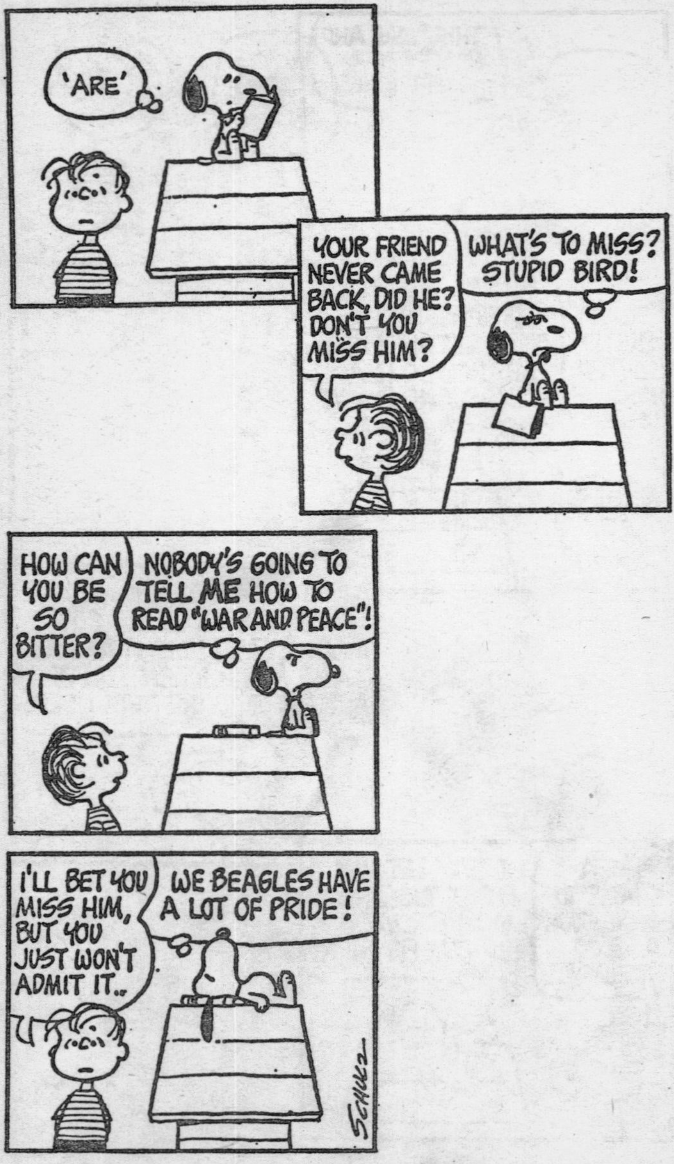
'ARE'
YOUR FRIEND NEVER CAME BACK, DID HE? DON'T YOU MISS HIM?
WHAT'S TO MISS? STUPID BIRD!
HOW CAN YOU BE SO BITTER?
NOBODY'S GOING TO TELL ME HOW TO READ "WAR AND PEACE"!
I'LL BET YOU MISS HIM, BUT YOU JUST WON'T ADMIT IT..
WE BEAGLES HAVE A LOT OF PRIDE!
SCHULZ

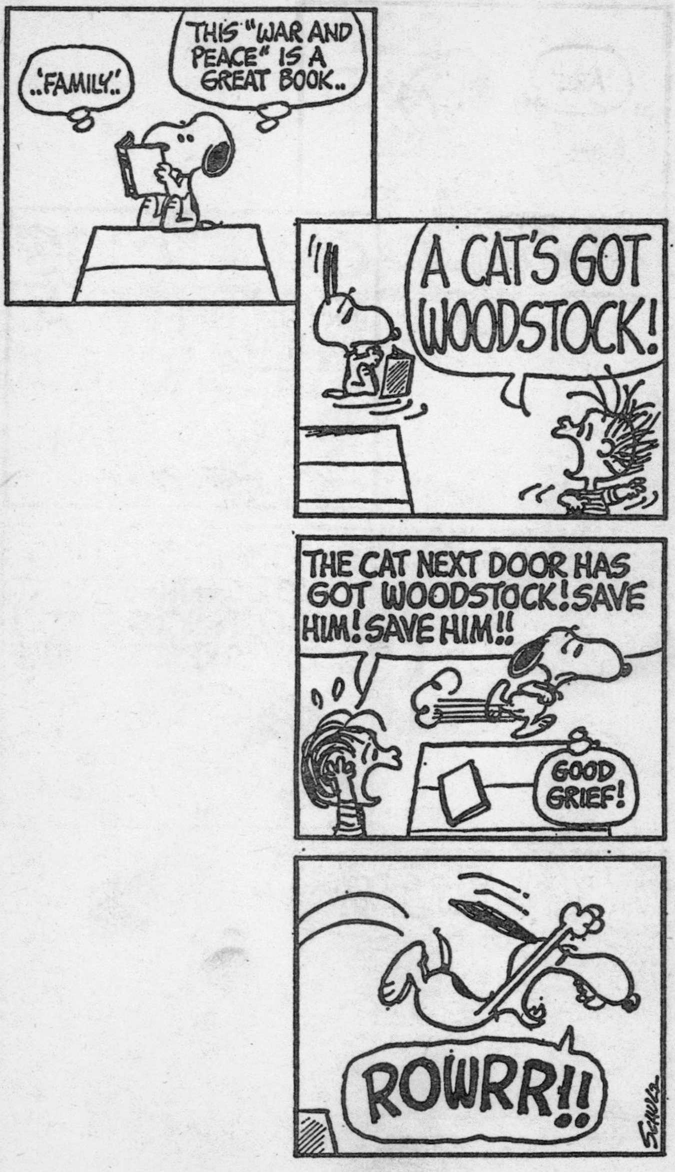
..'FAMILY.'..
THIS "WAR AND PEACE" IS A GREAT BOOK..
A CAT'S GOT WOODSTOCK!
THE CAT NEXT DOOR HAS GOT WOODSTOCK! SAVE HIM! SAVE HIM!!
GOOD GRIEF!
ROWRR!!
SCHULZ

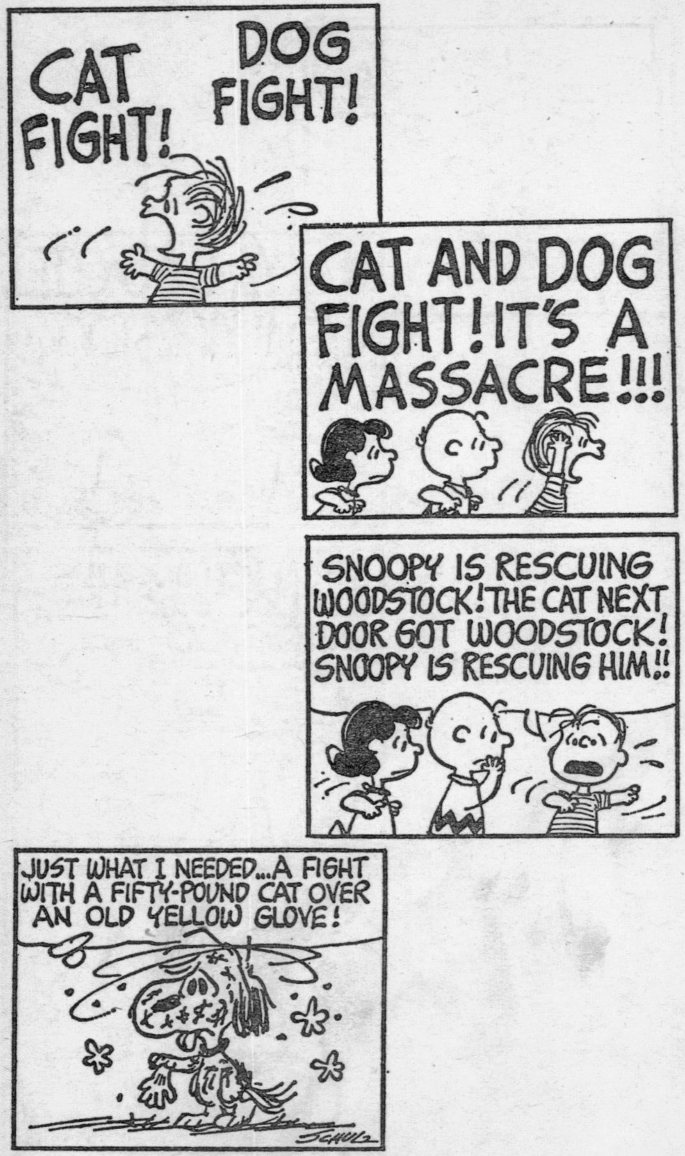
CAT FIGHT!
DOG FIGHT!
CAT AND DOG FIGHT! IT'S A MASSACRE!!!
SNOOPY IS RESCUING WOODSTOCK! THE CAT NEXT DOOR GOT WOODSTOCK! SNOOPY IS RESCUING HIM!!
JUST WHAT I NEEDED...A FIGHT WITH A FIFTY-POUND CAT OVER AN OLD YELLOW GLOVE!
SCHULZ

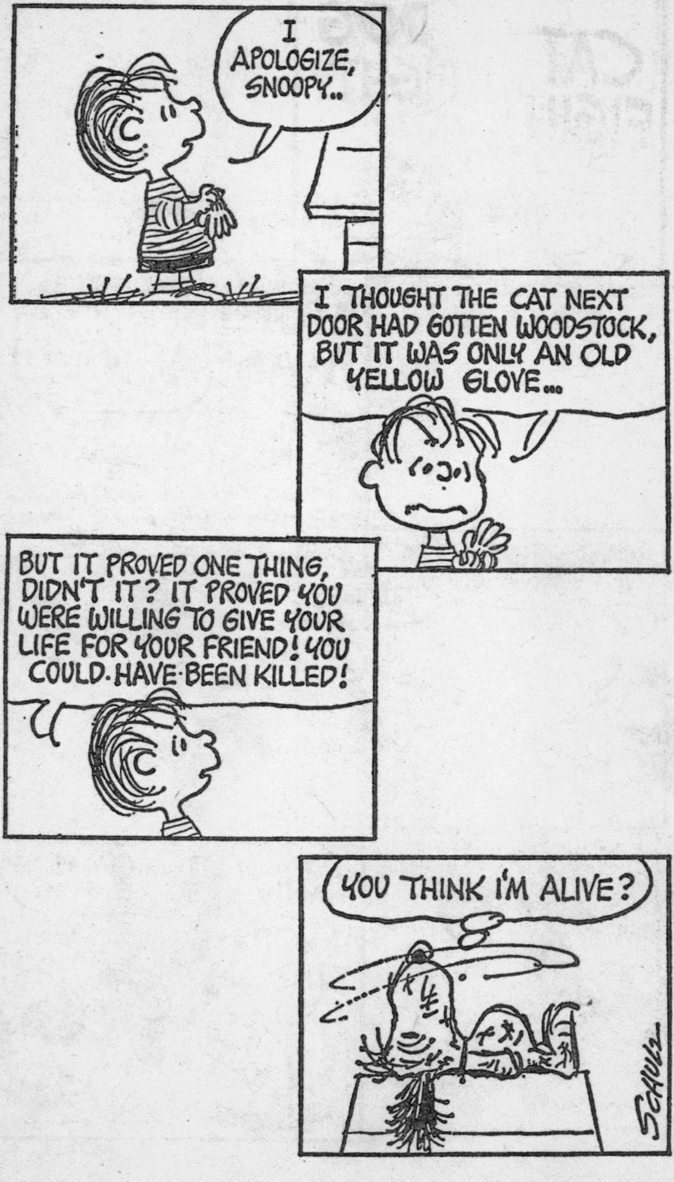
I APOLOGIZE, SNOOPY..
I THOUGHT THE CAT NEXT DOOR HAD GOTTEN WOODSTOCK, BUT IT WAS ONLY AN OLD YELLOW GLOVE...
BUT IT PROVED ONE THING, DIDN'T IT? IT PROVED YOU WERE WILLING TO GIVE YOUR LIFE FOR YOUR FRIEND! YOU COULD HAVE BEEN KILLED!
YOU THINK I'M ALIVE?
SCHULZ

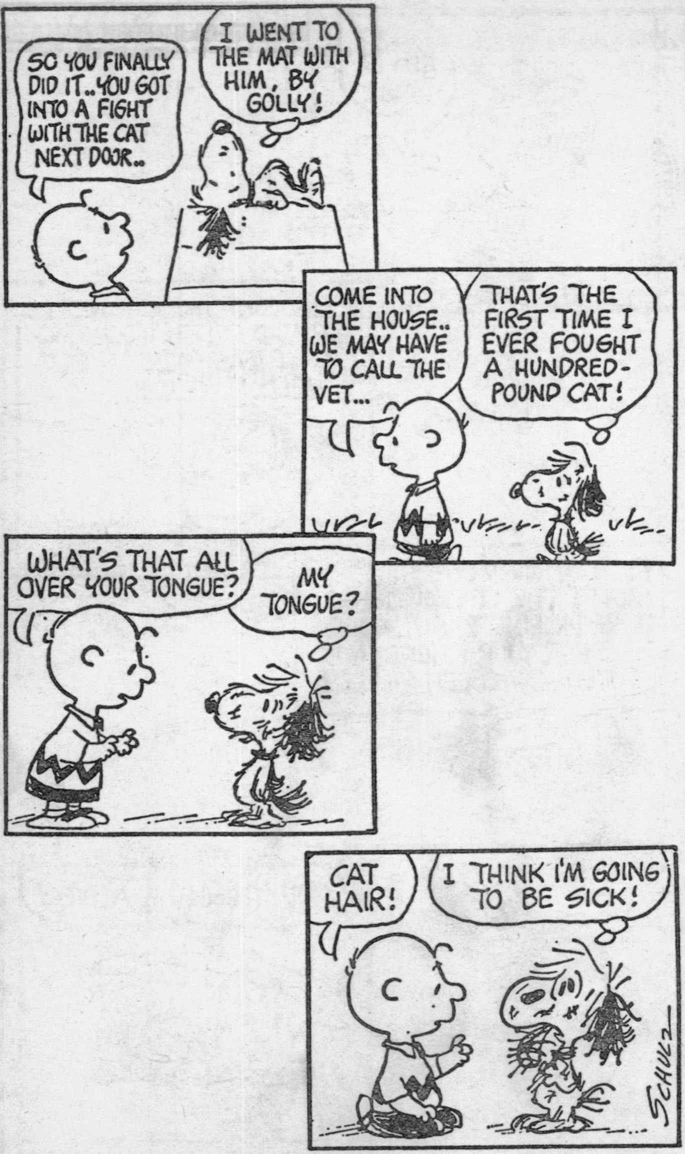
SO YOU FINALLY DID IT..YOU GOT INTO A FIGHT WITH THE CAT NEXT DOOR..
I WENT TO THE MAT WITH HIM, BY GOLLY!
COME INTO THE HOUSE.. WE MAY HAVE TO CALL THE VET...
THAT'S THE FIRST TIME I EVER FOUGHT A HUNDRED-POUND CAT!
WHAT'S THAT ALL OVER YOUR TONGUE?
MY TONGUE?
CAT HAIR!
I THINK I'M GOING TO BE SICK!
SCHULZ

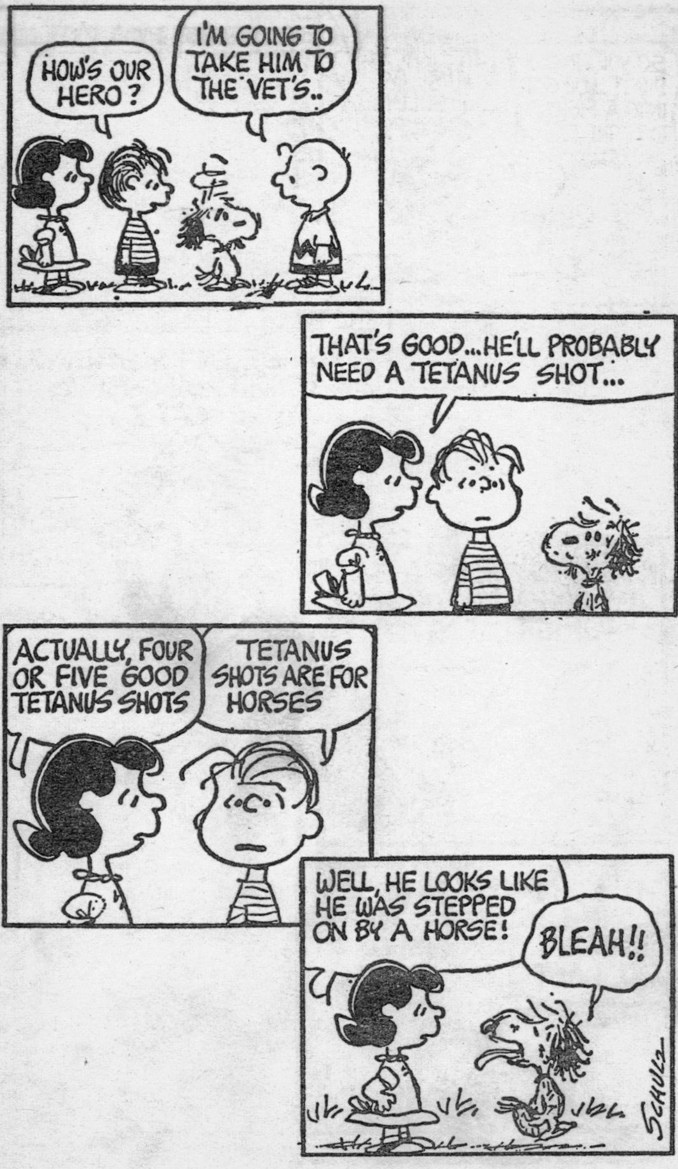
HOW'S OUR HERO?
I'M GOING TO TAKE HIM TO THE VET'S..
THAT'S GOOD...HE'LL PROBABLY NEED A TETANUS SHOT...
ACTUALLY, FOUR OR FIVE GOOD TETANUS SHOTS
TETANUS SHOTS ARE FOR HORSES
WELL, HE LOOKS LIKE HE WAS STEPPED ON BY A HORSE!
BLEAH!!
SCHULZ

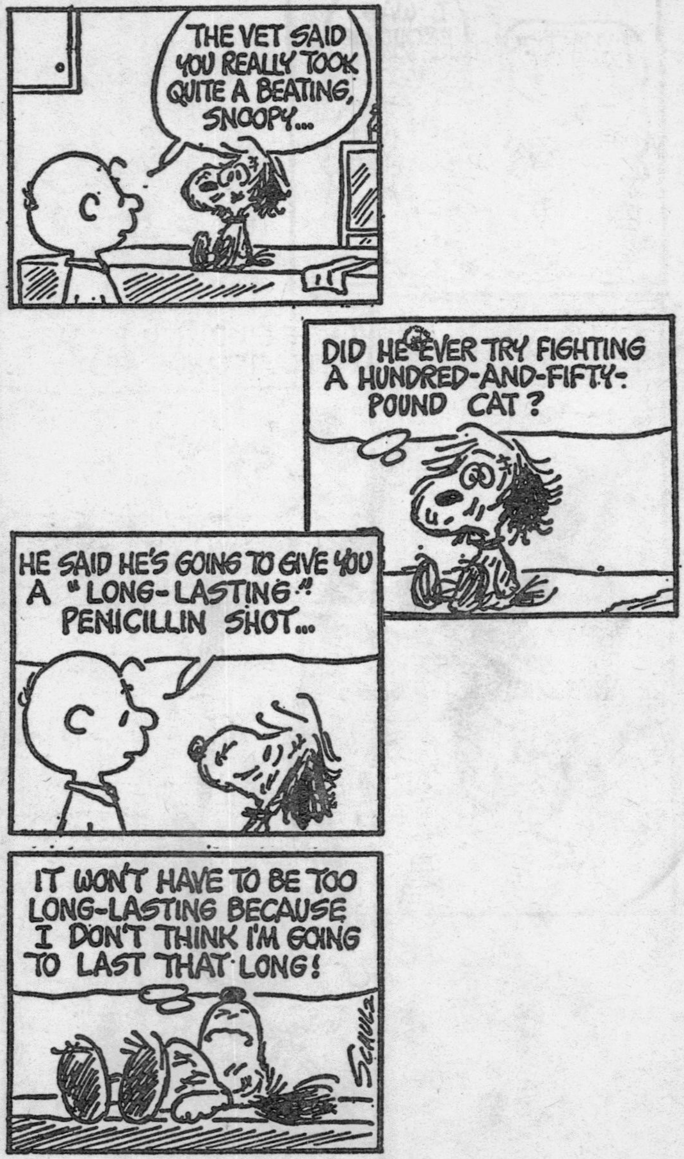
THE VET SAID YOU REALLY TOOK QUITE A BEATING, SNOOPY...
DID HE EVER TRY FIGHTING A HUNDRED-AND-FIFTY-POUND CAT?
HE SAID HE'S GOING TO GIVE YOU A "LONG-LASTING" PENICILLIN SHOT...
IT WON'T HAVE TO BE TOO LONG-LASTING BECAUSE I DON'T THINK I'M GOING TO LAST THAT LONG!
SCHULZ

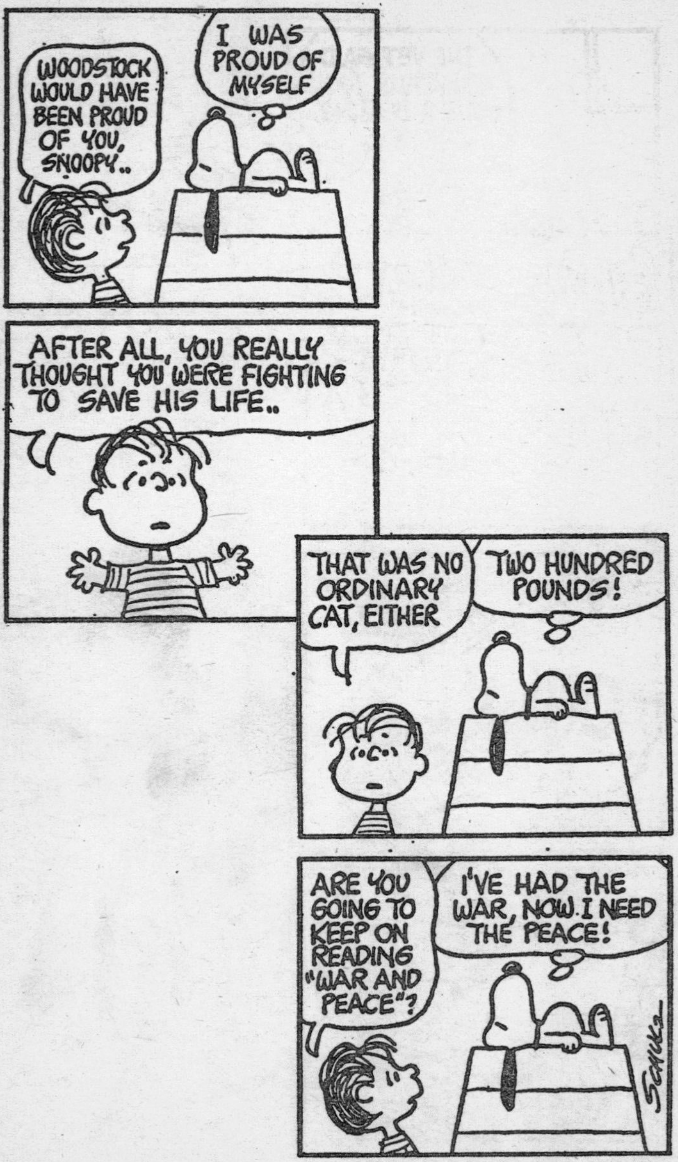
WOODSTOCK WOULD HAVE BEEN PROUD OF YOU, SNOOPY..
I WAS PROUD OF MYSELF
AFTER ALL, YOU REALLY THOUGHT YOU WERE FIGHTING TO SAVE HIS LIFE..
THAT WAS NO ORDINARY CAT, EITHER
TWO HUNDRED POUNDS!
ARE YOU GOING TO KEEP ON READING "WAR AND PEACE"?
I'VE HAD THE WAR, NOW. I NEED THE PEACE!
SCHULZ

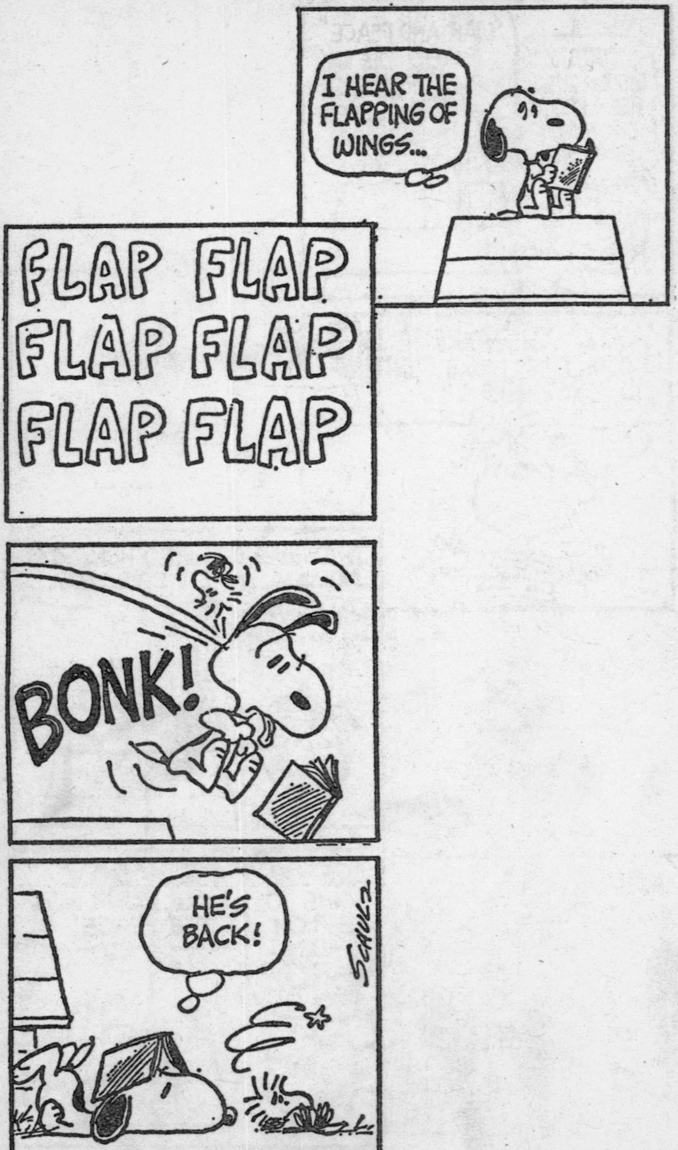
I HEAR THE FLAPPING OF WINGS...
FLAP FLAP FLAP FLAP FLAP FLAP
BONK!
HE'S BACK!
SCHULZ

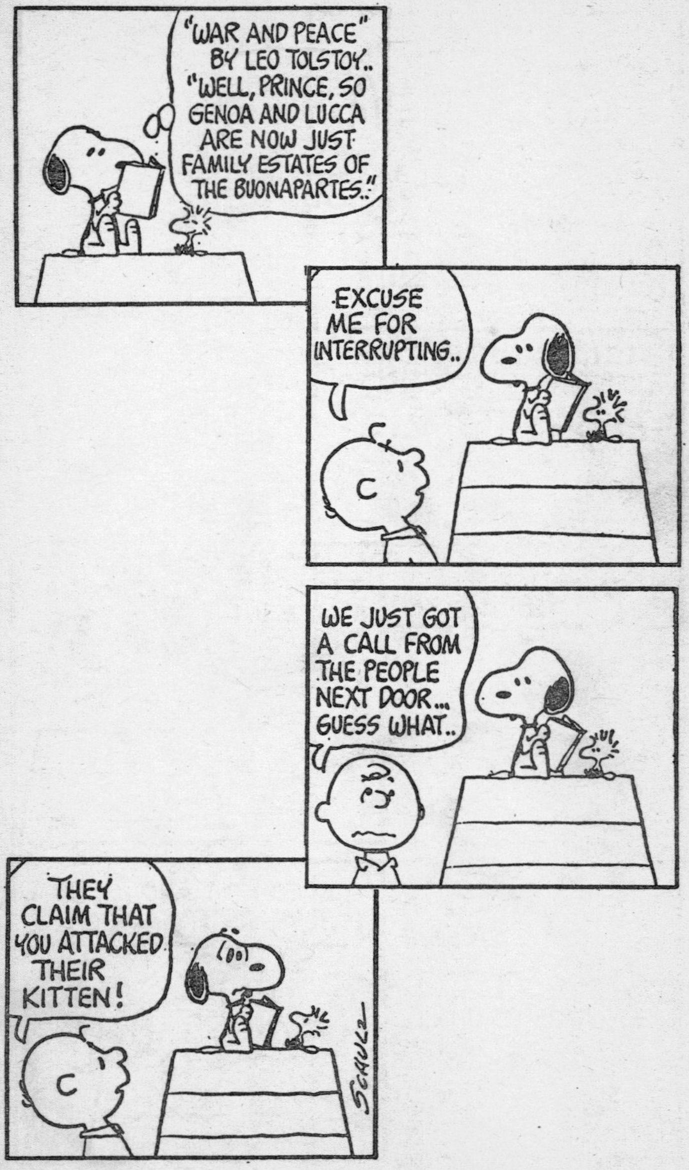
"WAR AND PEACE" BY LEO TOLSTOY.. "WELL, PRINCE, SO GENOA AND LUCCA ARE NOW JUST FAMILY ESTATES OF THE BUONAPARTES."
EXCUSE ME FOR INTERRUPTING..
WE JUST GOT A CALL FROM THE PEOPLE NEXT DOOR... GUESS WHAT..
THEY CLAIM THAT YOU ATTACKED THEIR KITTEN!
SCHULZ

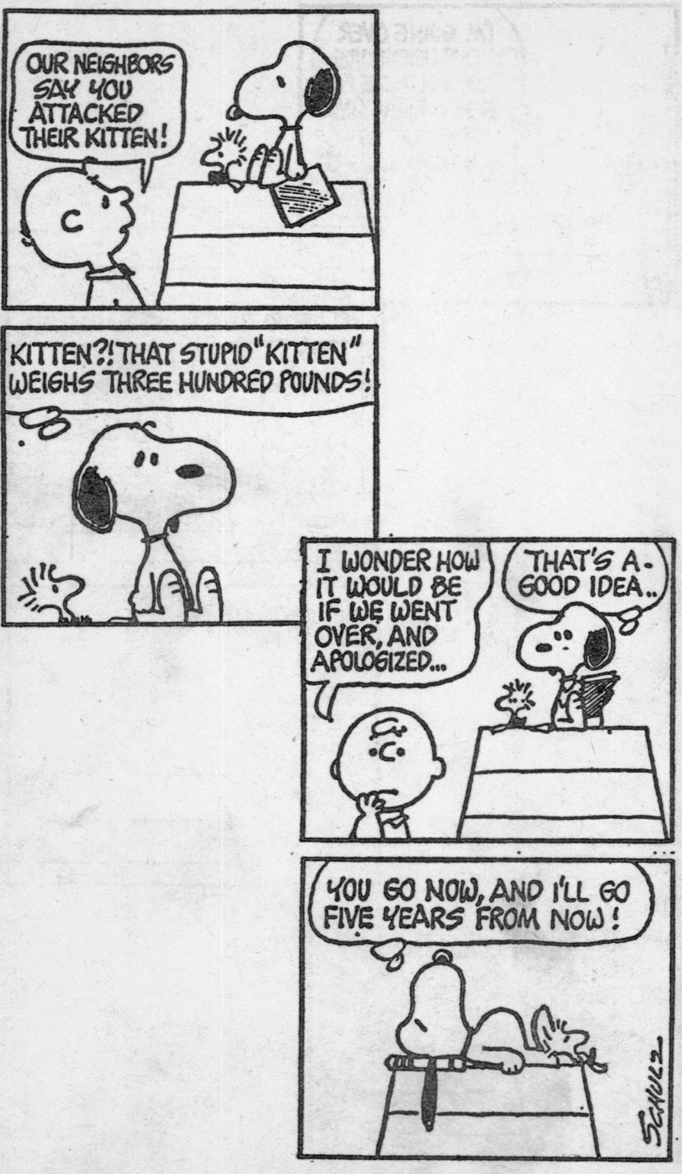
OUR NEIGHBORS SAY YOU ATTACKED THEIR KITTEN!
KITTEN?! THAT STUPID "KITTEN" WEIGHS THREE HUNDRED POUNDS!
I WONDER HOW IT WOULD BE IF WE WENT OVER, AND APOLOGIZED...
THAT'S A GOOD IDEA..
YOU GO NOW, AND I'LL GO FIVE YEARS FROM NOW!
SCHULZ

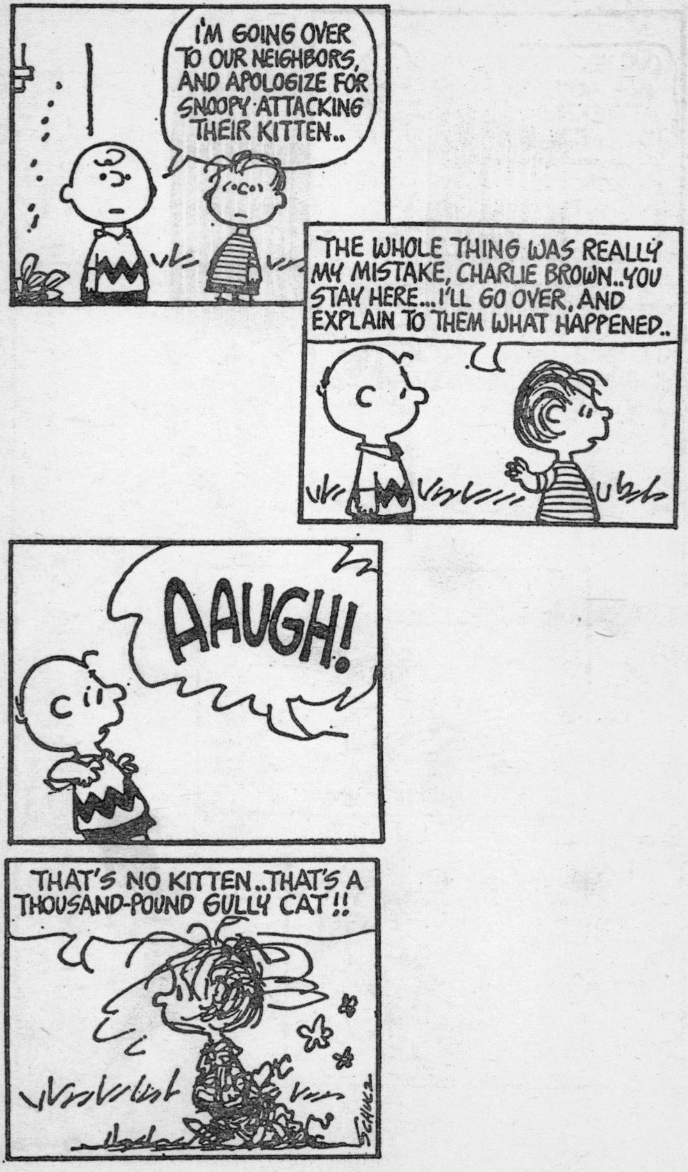
I'M GOING OVER TO OUR NEIGHBORS, AND APOLOGIZE FOR SNOOPY ATTACKING THEIR KITTEN..
THE WHOLE THING WAS REALLY MY MISTAKE, CHARLIE BROWN..YOU STAY HERE...I'LL GO OVER, AND EXPLAIN TO THEM WHAT HAPPENED..
AAUGH!
THAT'S NO KITTEN..THAT'S A THOUSAND-POUND GULLY CAT!!
SCHULZ

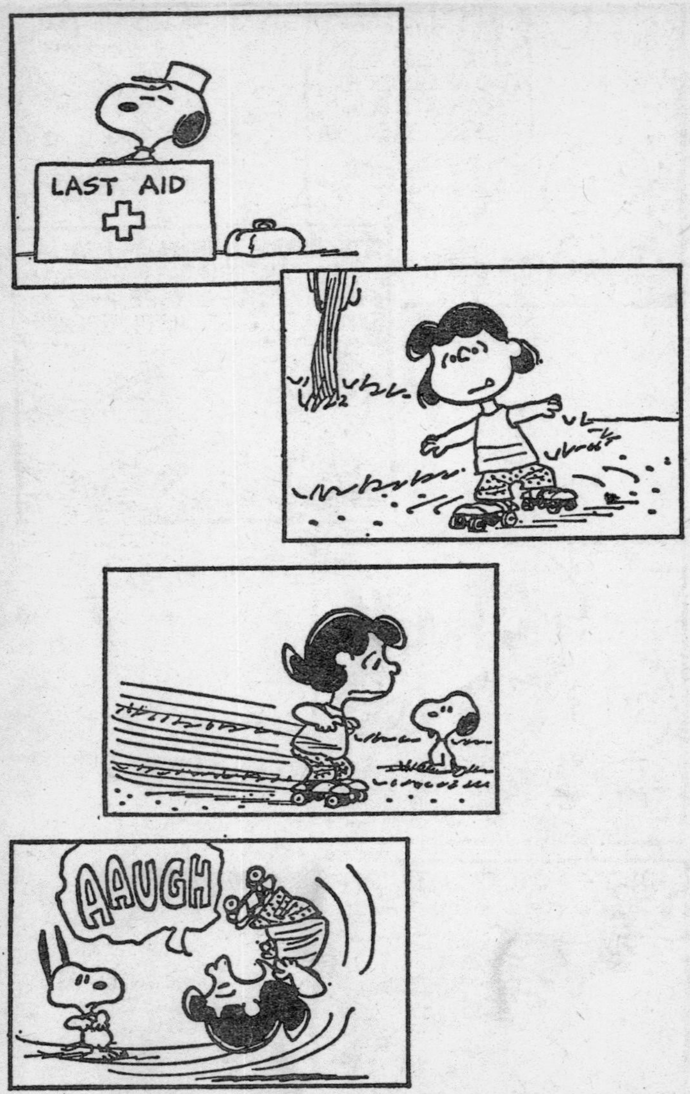
LAST AID
AAUGH

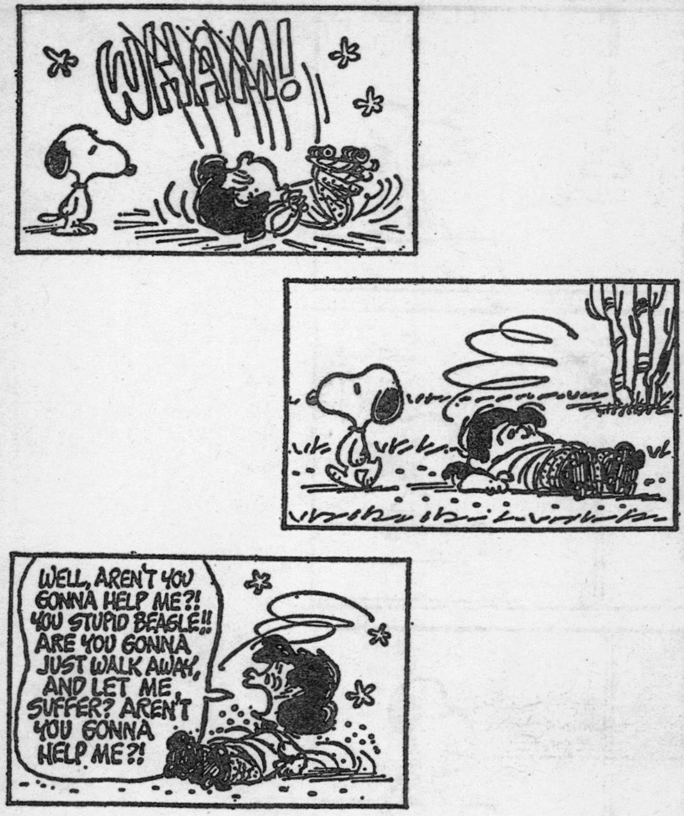
WHAM!
WELL, AREN'T YOU GONNA HELP ME?! YOU STUPID BEAGLE!! ARE YOU GONNA JUST WALK AWAY, AND LET ME SUFFER? AREN'T YOU GONNA HELP ME?!
I HAVE NO DESIRE TO LEAVE MYSELF OPEN FOR A MALPRACTICE SUIT!
SCHULZ

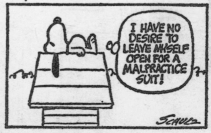

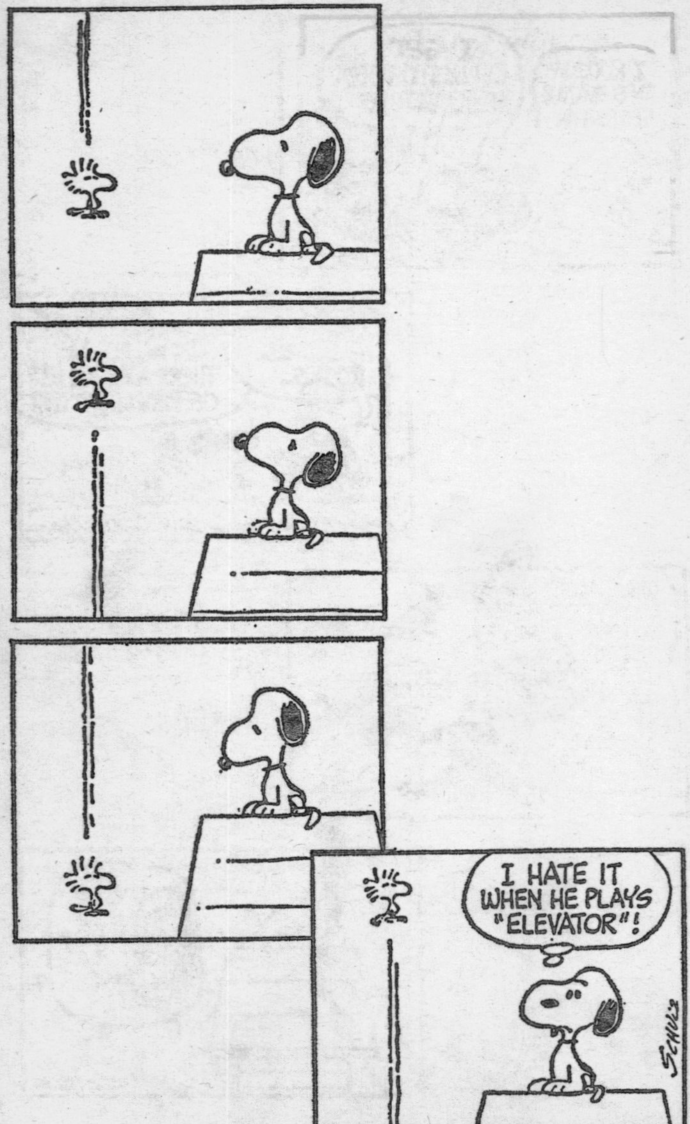
I HATE IT WHEN HE PLAYS "ELEVATOR"!
SCHULZ

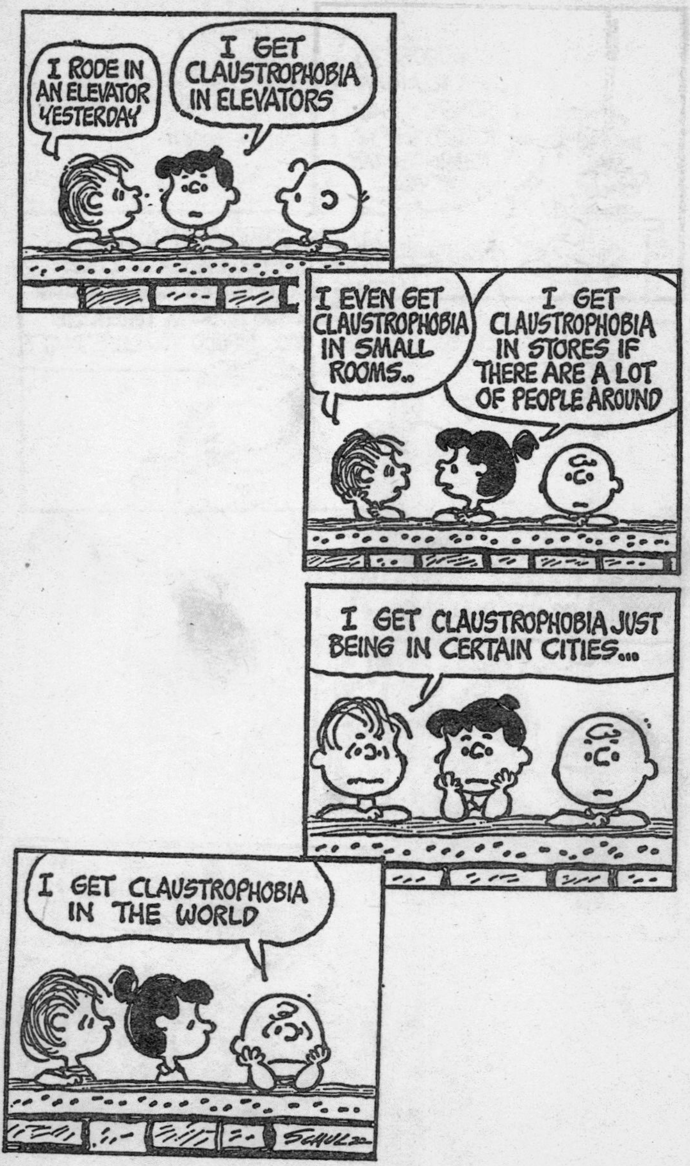

I RODE IN AN ELEVATOR YESTERDAY
I GET CLAUSTROPHOBIA IN ELEVATORS
I EVEN GET CLAUSTROPHOBIA IN SMALL ROOMS..
I GET CLAUSTROPHOBIA IN STORES IF THERE ARE A LOT OF PEOPLE AROUND
I GET CLAUSTROPHOBIA JUST BEING IN CERTAIN CITIES...
I GET CLAUSTROPHOBIA IN THE WORLD
SCHULZ

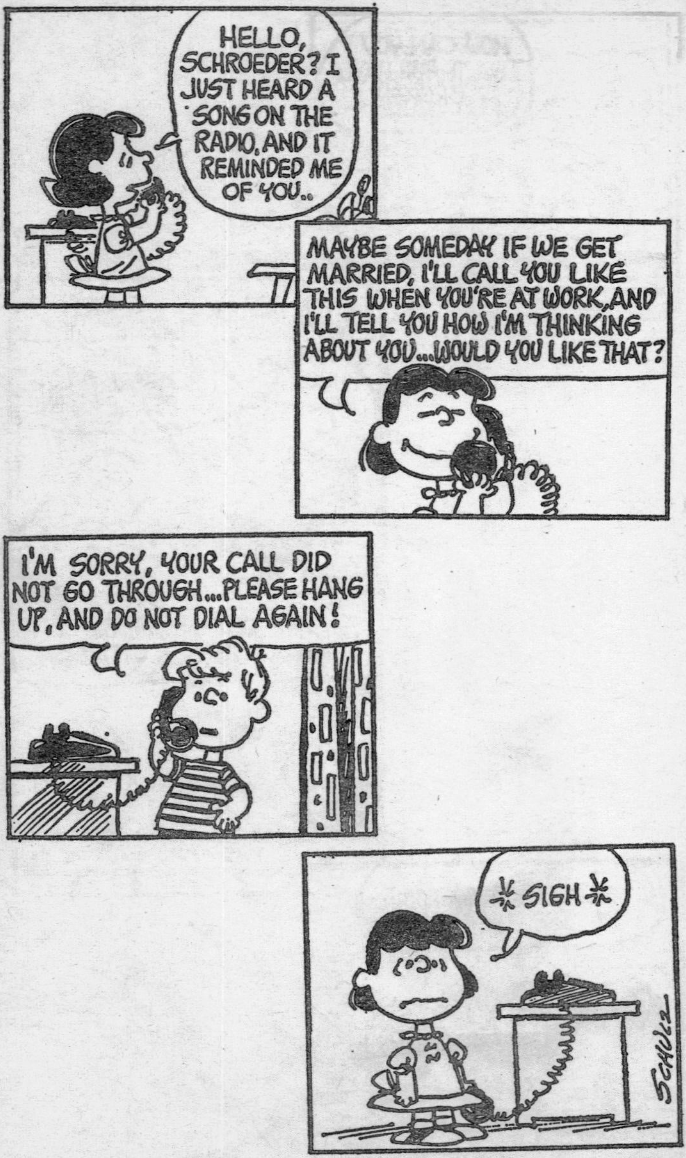
HELLO, SCHROEDER? I JUST HEARD A SONG ON THE RADIO, AND IT REMINDED ME OF YOU..
MAYBE SOMEDAY IF WE GET MARRIED, I'LL CALL YOU LIKE THIS WHEN YOU'RE AT WORK, AND I'LL TELL YOU HOW I'M THINKING ABOUT YOU...WOULD YOU LIKE THAT?
I'M SORRY, YOUR CALL DID NOT GO THROUGH...PLEASE HANG UP, AND DO NOT DIAL AGAIN!
* SIGH *
SCHULZ

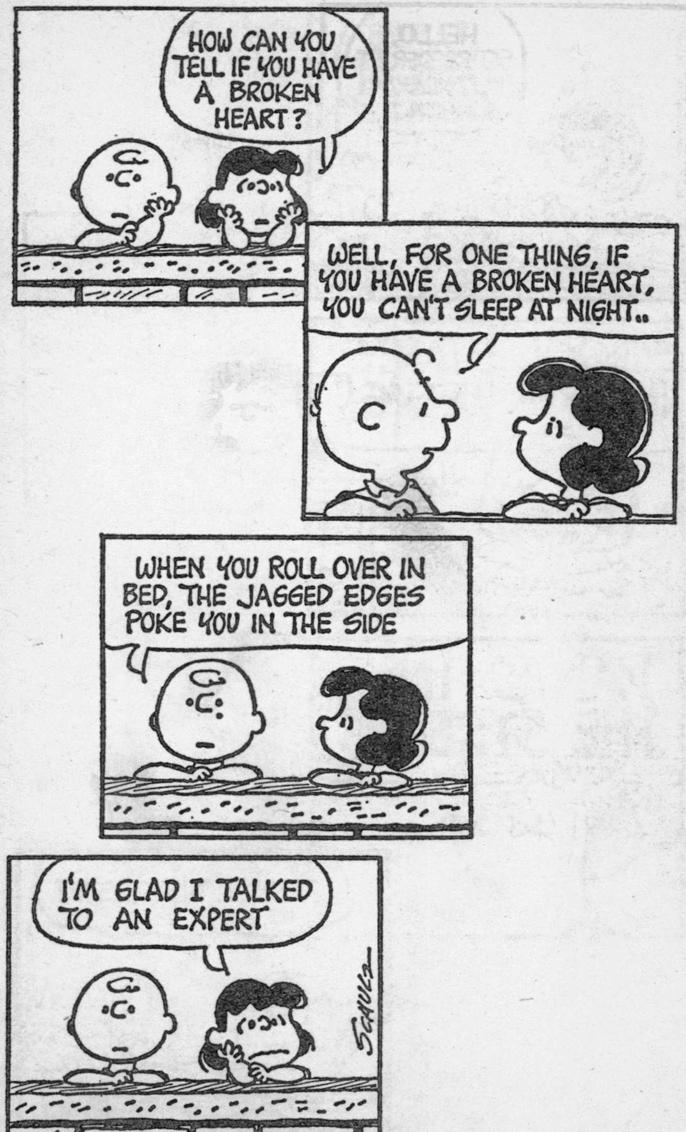
HOW CAN YOU TELL IF YOU HAVE A BROKEN HEART?
WELL, FOR ONE THING, IF YOU HAVE A BROKEN HEART, YOU CAN'T SLEEP AT NIGHT..
WHEN YOU ROLL OVER IN BED, THE JAGGED EDGES POKE YOU IN THE SIDE
I'M GLAD I TALKED TO AN EXPERT
SCHULZ

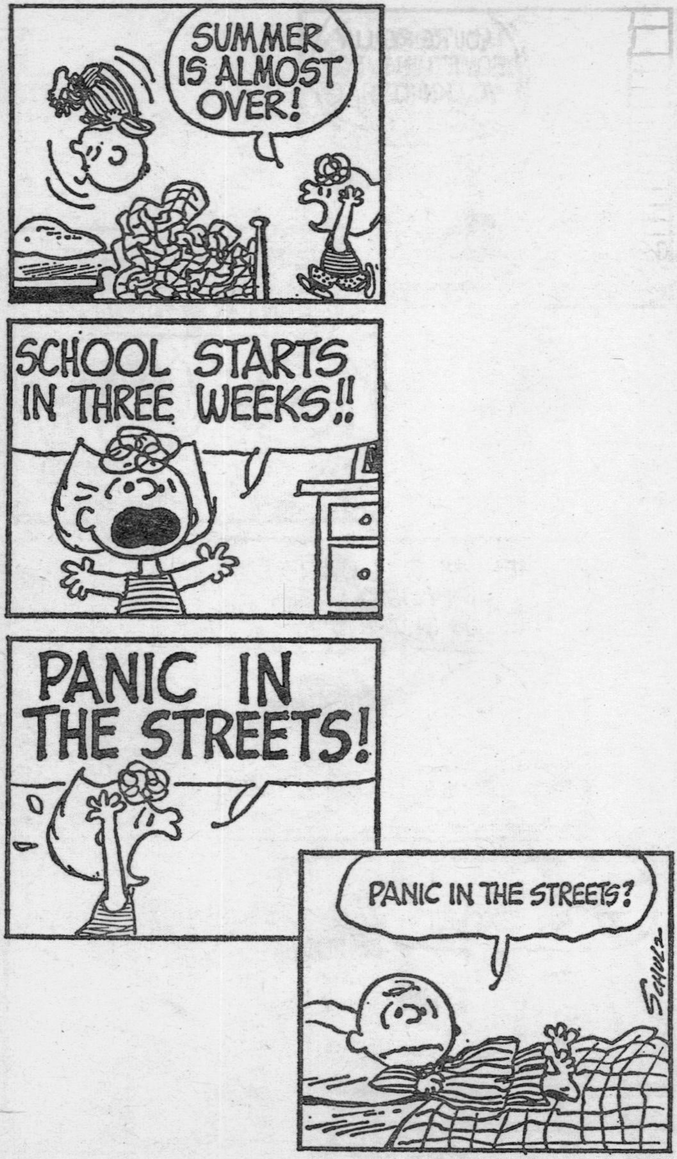
SUMMER IS ALMOST OVER!
SCHOOL STARTS IN THREE WEEKS!!
PANIC IN THE STREETS!
PANIC IN THE STREETS?
SCHULZ

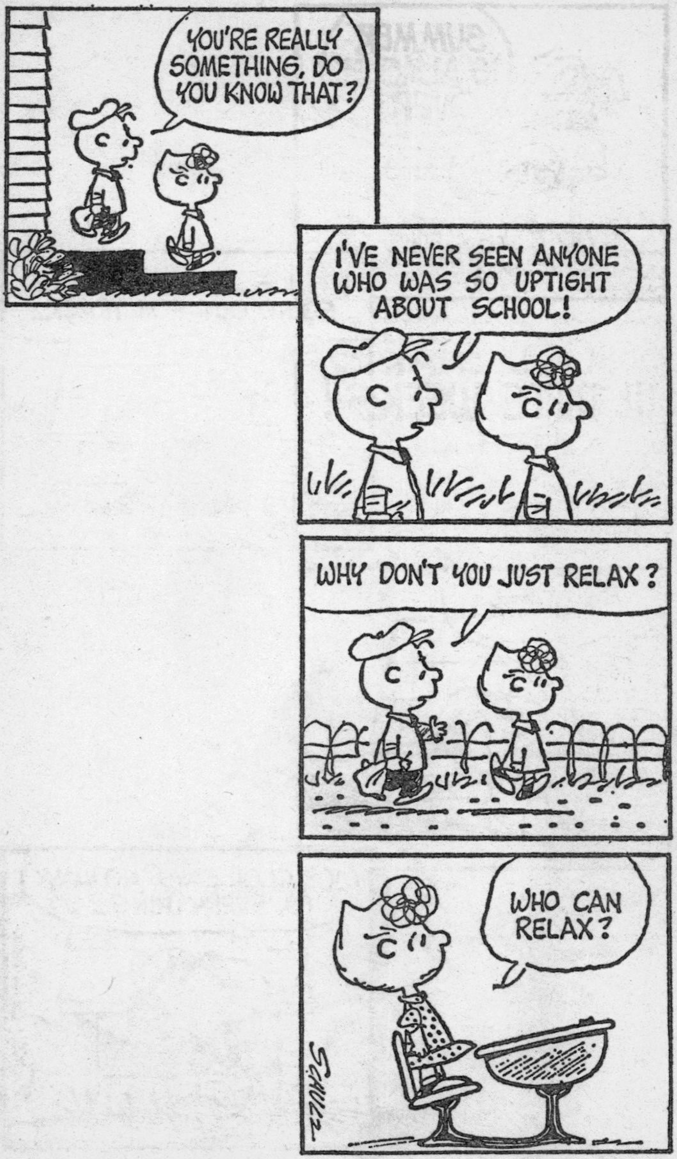
YOU'RE REALLY SOMETHING, DO YOU KNOW THAT?
I'VE NEVER SEEN ANYONE WHO WAS SO UPTIGHT ABOUT SCHOOL!
WHY DON'T YOU JUST RELAX?
WHO CAN RELAX?
SCHULZ

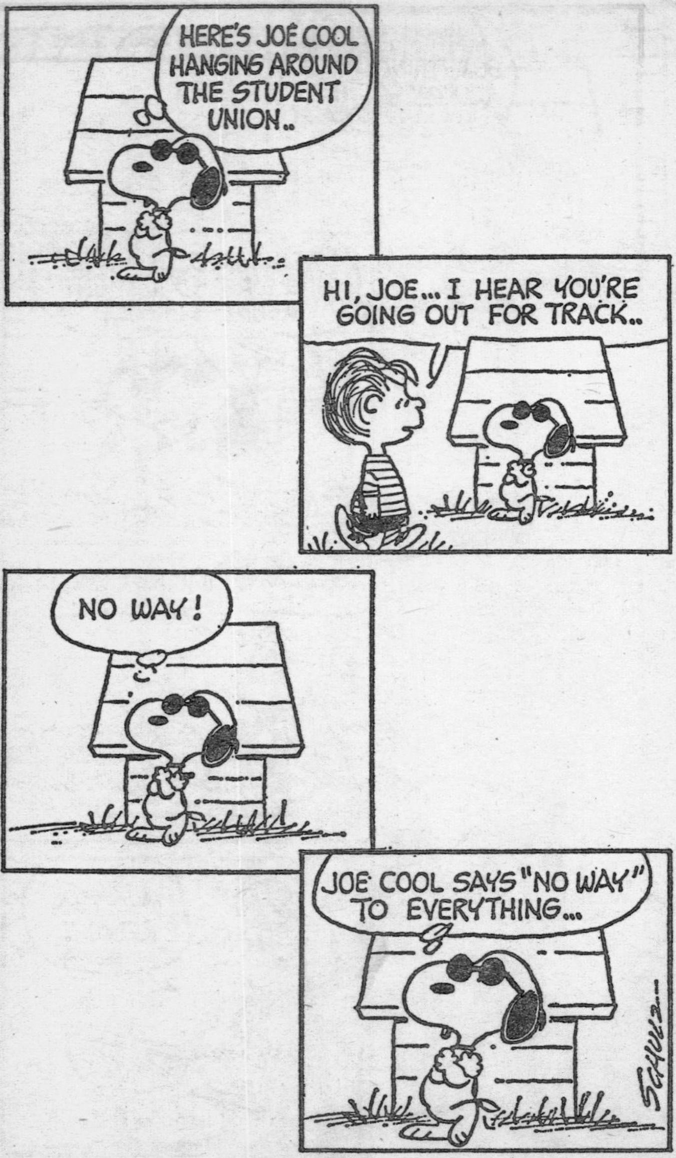
HERE'S JOE COOL HANGING AROUND THE STUDENT UNION..
HI, JOE... I HEAR YOU'RE GOING OUT FOR TRACK..
NO WAY!
JOE COOL SAYS "NO WAY" TO EVERYTHING...
SCHULZ

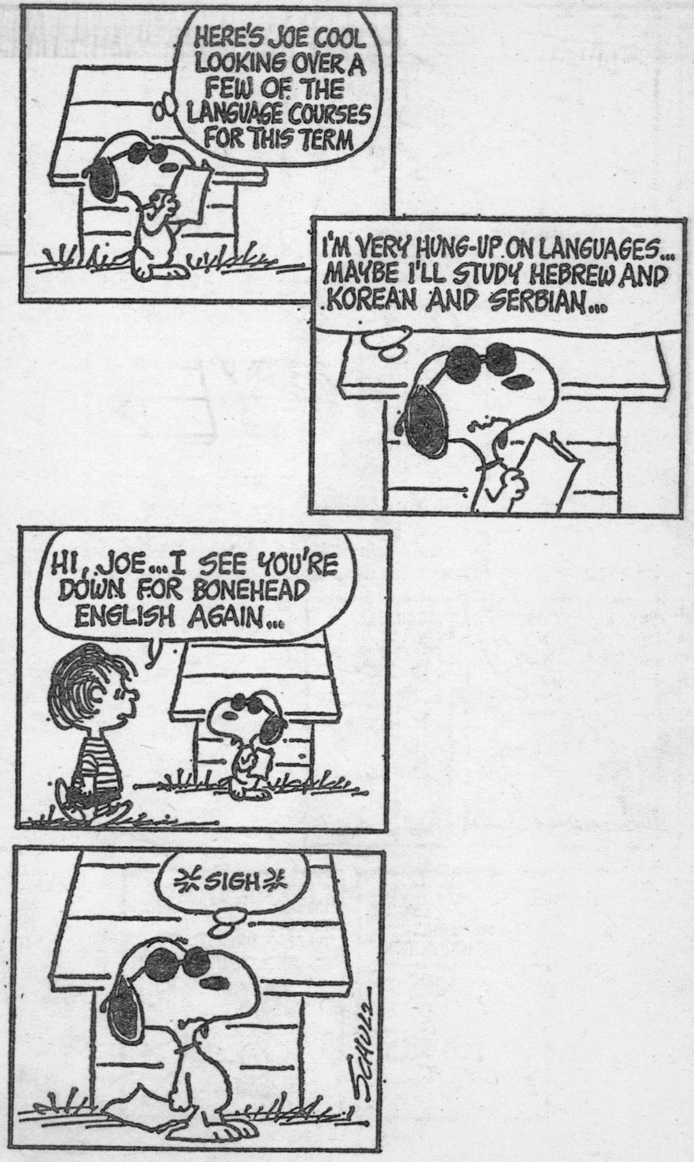
HERE'S JOE COOL LOOKING OVER A FEW OF THE LANGUAGE COURSES FOR THIS TERM
I'M VERY HUNG-UP ON LANGUAGES... MAYBE I'LL STUDY HEBREW AND KOREAN AND SERBIAN...
HI, JOE...I SEE YOU'RE DOWN FOR BONEHEAD ENGLISH AGAIN...
SIGH
SCHULZ

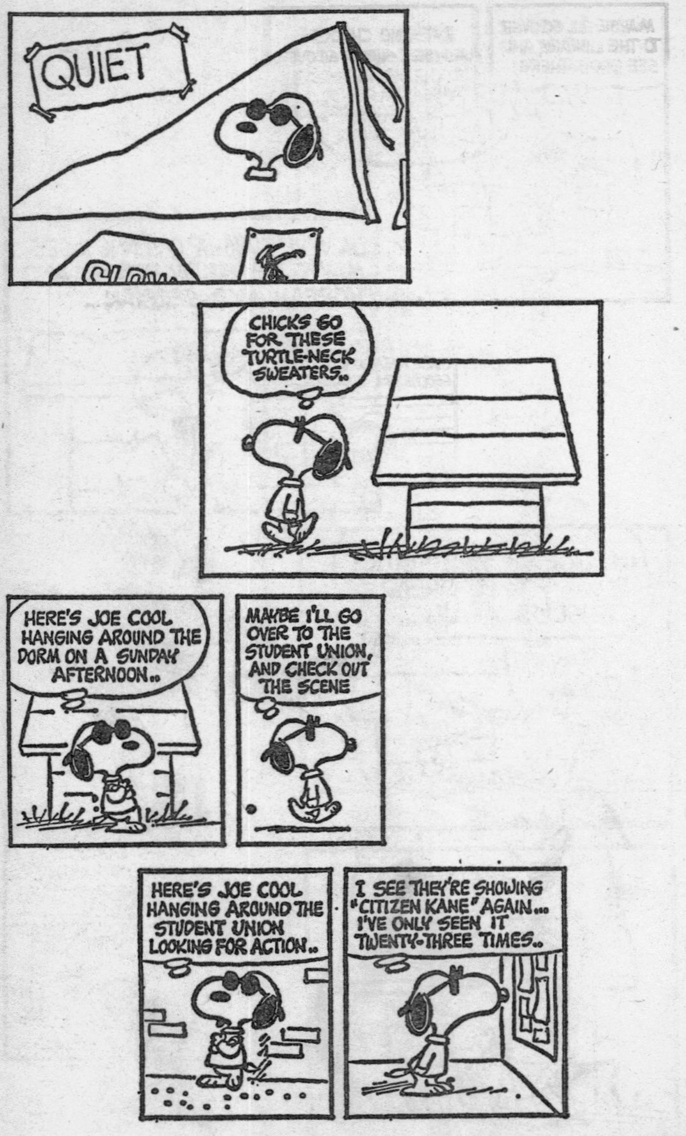
QUIET
CHICKS GO FOR THESE TURTLE-NECK SWEATERS..
HERE'S JOE COOL HANGING AROUND THE DORM ON A SUNDAY AFTERNOON..
MAYBE I'LL GO OVER TO THE STUDENT UNION, AND CHECK OUT THE SCENE
HERE'S JOE COOL HANGING AROUND THE STUDENT UNION LOOKING FOR ACTION..
I SEE THEY'RE SHOWING "CITIZEN KANE" AGAIN... I'VE ONLY SEEN IT TWENTY-THREE TIMES..

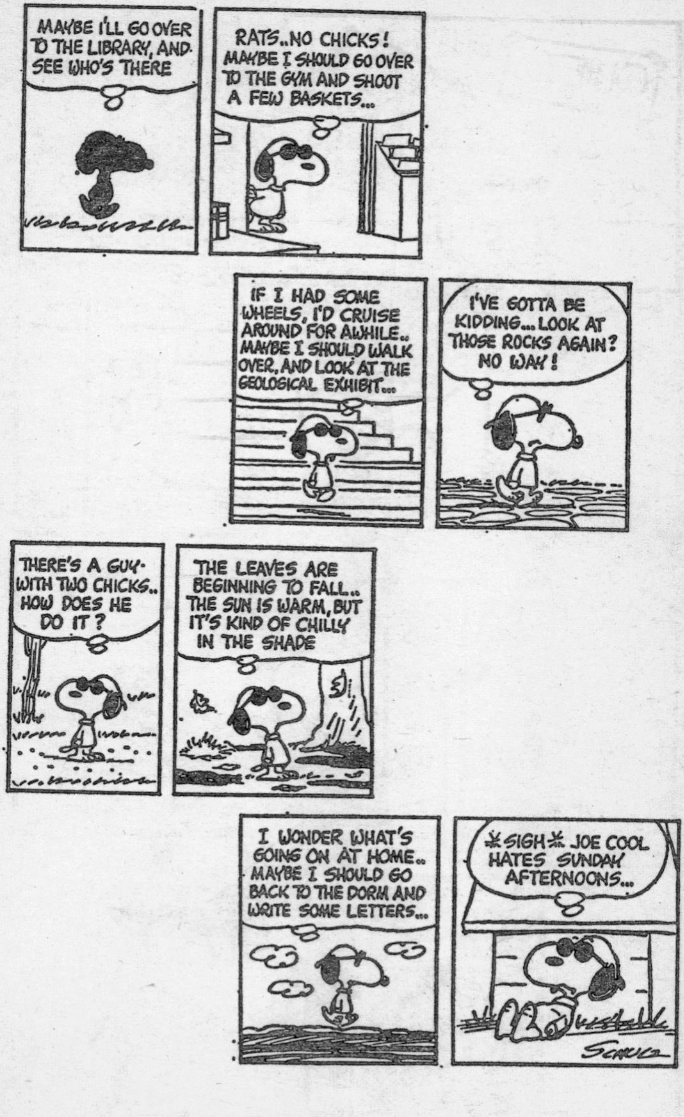
MAYBE I'LL GO OVER TO THE LIBRARY, AND SEE WHO'S THERE
RATS..NO CHICKS! MAYBE I SHOULD GO OVER TO THE GYM AND SHOOT A FEW BASKETS...
IF I HAD SOME WHEELS, I'D CRUISE AROUND FOR AWHILE.. MAYBE I SHOULD WALK OVER, AND LOOK AT THE GEOLOGICAL EXHIBIT...
I'VE GOTTA BE KIDDING... LOOK AT THOSE ROCKS AGAIN? NO WAY!
THERE'S A GUY WITH TWO CHICKS.. HOW DOES HE DO IT?
THE LEAVES ARE BEGINNING TO FALL.. THE SUN IS WARM, BUT IT'S KIND OF CHILLY IN THE SHADE
I WONDER WHAT'S GOING ON AT HOME.. MAYBE I SHOULD GO BACK TO THE DORM AND WRITE SOME LETTERS...
SIGH JOE COOL HATES SUNDAY AFTERNOONS...
SCHULZ

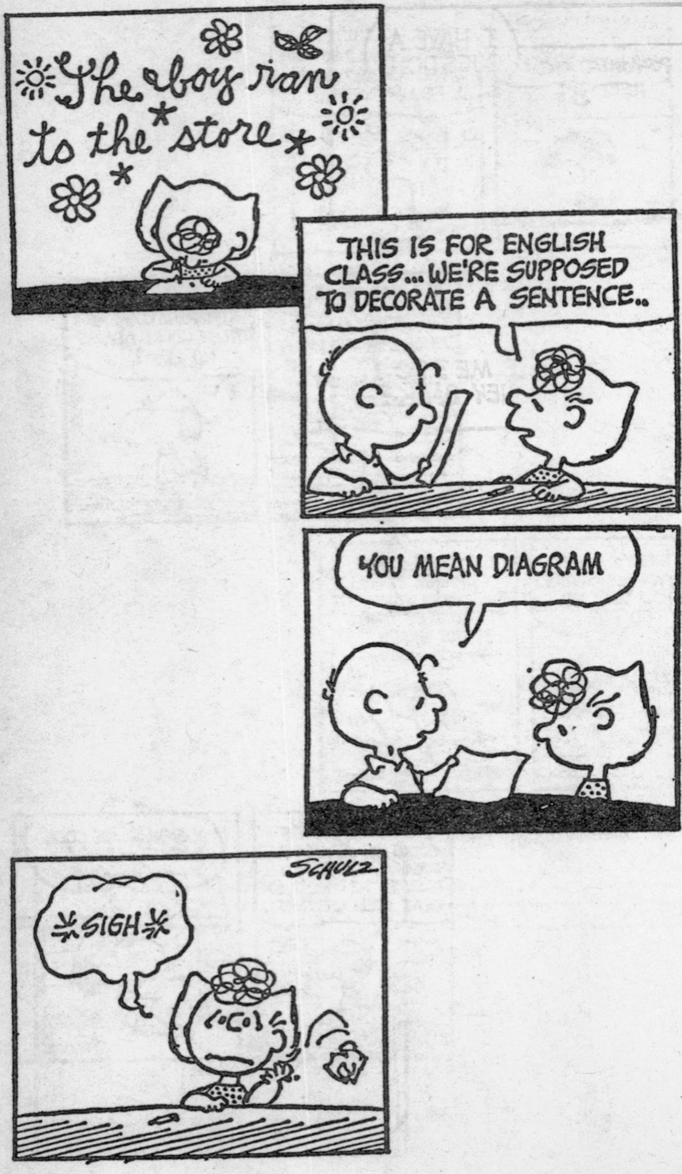
The boy ran to the store
THIS IS FOR ENGLISH CLASS... WE'RE SUPPOSED TO DECORATE A SENTENCE..
YOU MEAN DIAGRAM
SCHULZ
SIGH

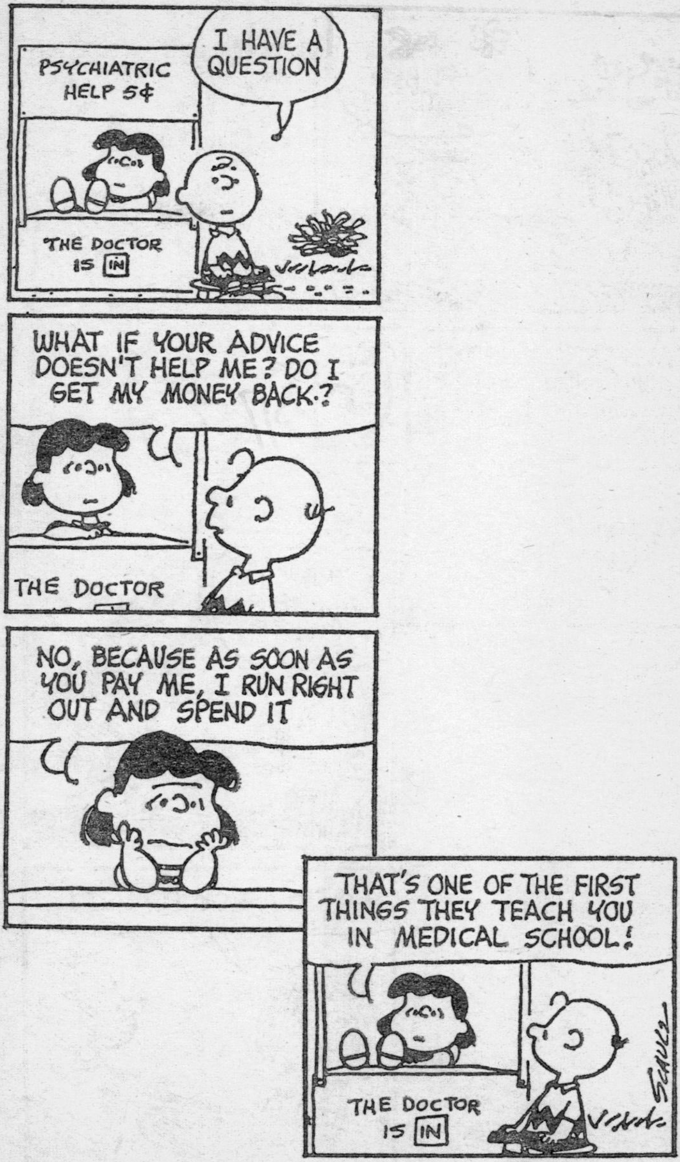
PSYCHIATRIC HELP 5¢
I HAVE A QUESTION
THE DOCTOR IS IN
WHAT IF YOUR ADVICE DOESN'T HELP ME? DO I GET MY MONEY BACK.?
THE DOCTOR
NO, BECAUSE AS SOON AS YOU PAY ME, I RUN RIGHT OUT AND SPEND IT
THAT'S ONE OF THE FIRST THINGS THEY TEACH YOU IN MEDICAL SCHOOL!
THE DOCTOR IS IN
SCHULZ

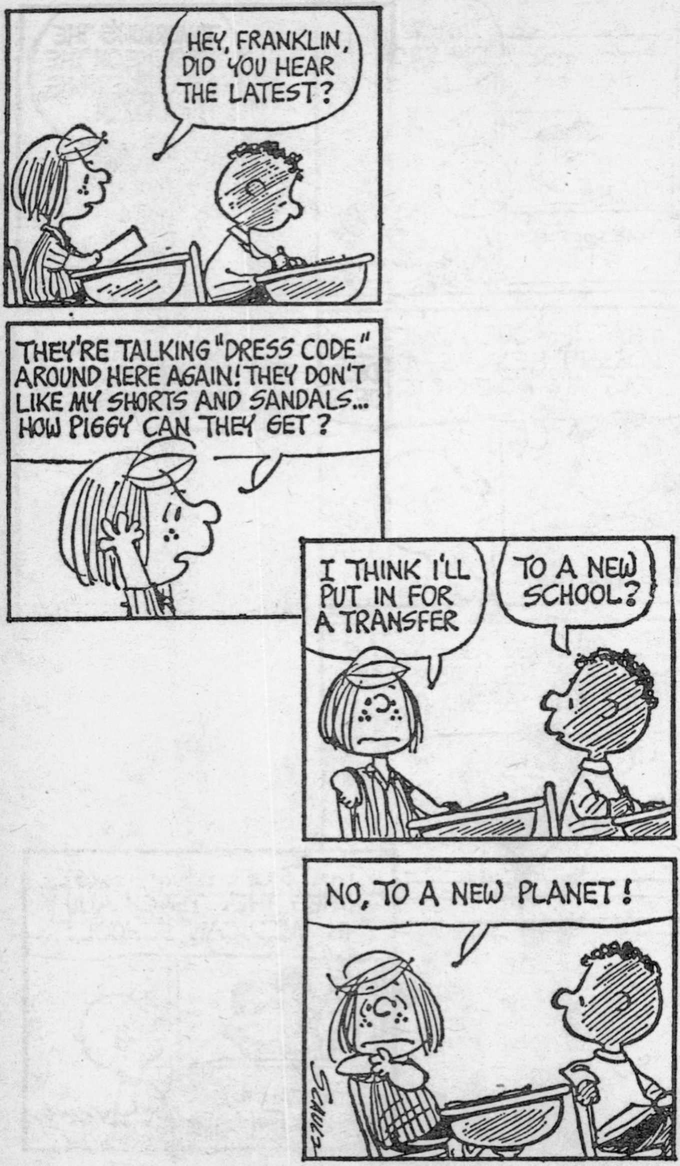
HEY, FRANKLIN, DID YOU HEAR THE LATEST?
THEY'RE TALKING "DRESS CODE" AROUND HERE AGAIN! THEY DON'T LIKE MY SHORTS AND SANDALS... HOW PIGGY CAN THEY GET?
I THINK I'LL PUT IN FOR A TRANSFER
TO A NEW SCHOOL?
NO, TO A NEW PLANET!
SCHULZ

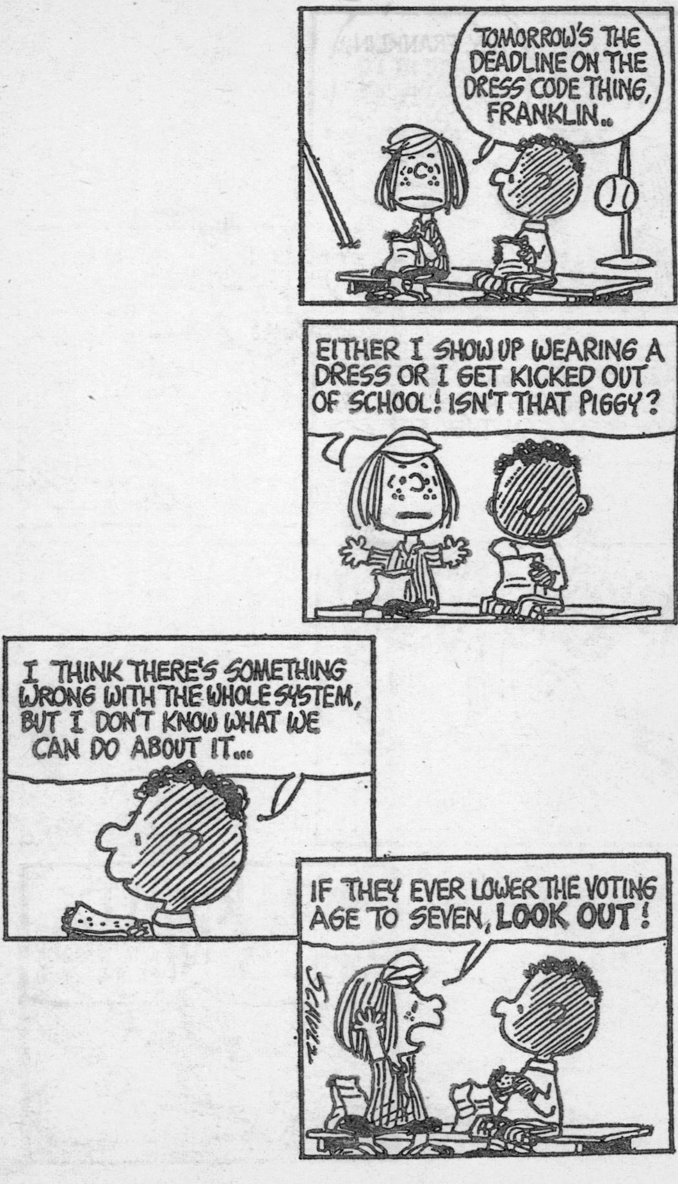
TOMORROW'S THE DEADLINE ON THE DRESS CODE THING, FRANKLIN..
EITHER I SHOW UP WEARING A DRESS OR I GET KICKED OUT OF SCHOOL! ISN'T THAT PIGGY?
I THINK THERE'S SOMETHING WRONG WITH THE WHOLE SYSTEM, BUT I DON'T KNOW WHAT WE CAN DO ABOUT IT...
IF THEY EVER LOWER THE VOTING AGE TO SEVEN, LOOK OUT!
SCHULZ

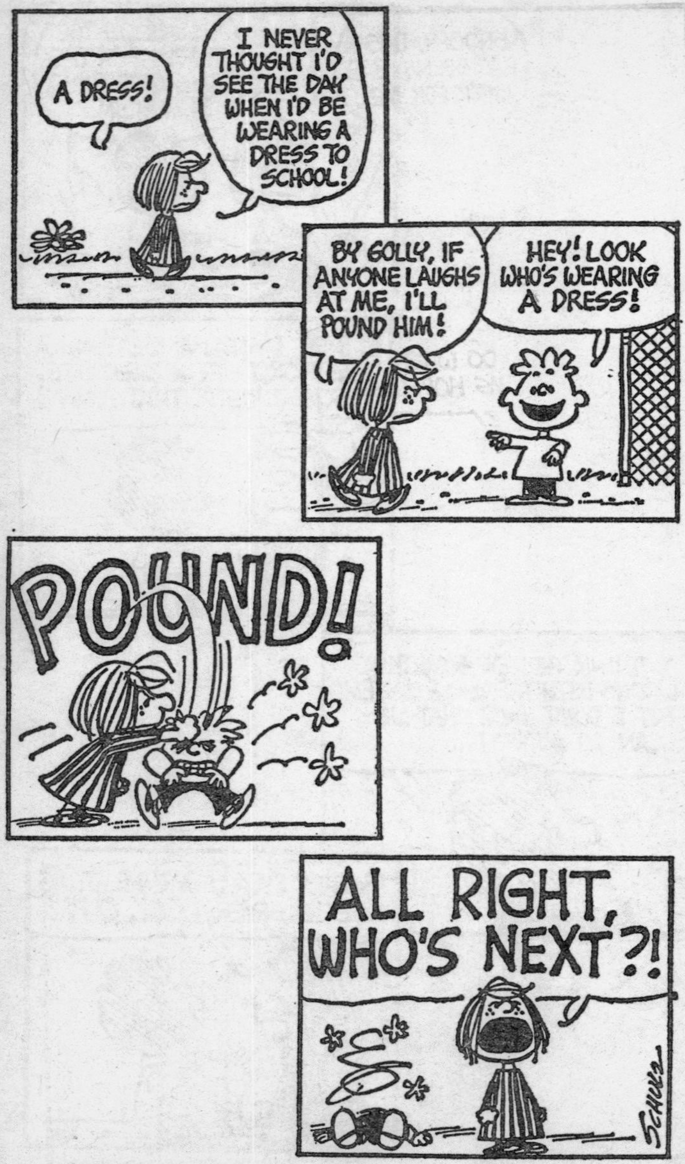
A DRESS!
I NEVER THOUGHT I'D SEE THE DAY WHEN I'D BE WEARING A DRESS TO SCHOOL!
BY GOLLY, IF ANYONE LAUGHS AT ME, I'LL POUND HIM!
HEY! LOOK WHO'S WEARING A DRESS!
POUND!
ALL RIGHT, WHO'S NEXT?!
SCHULZ

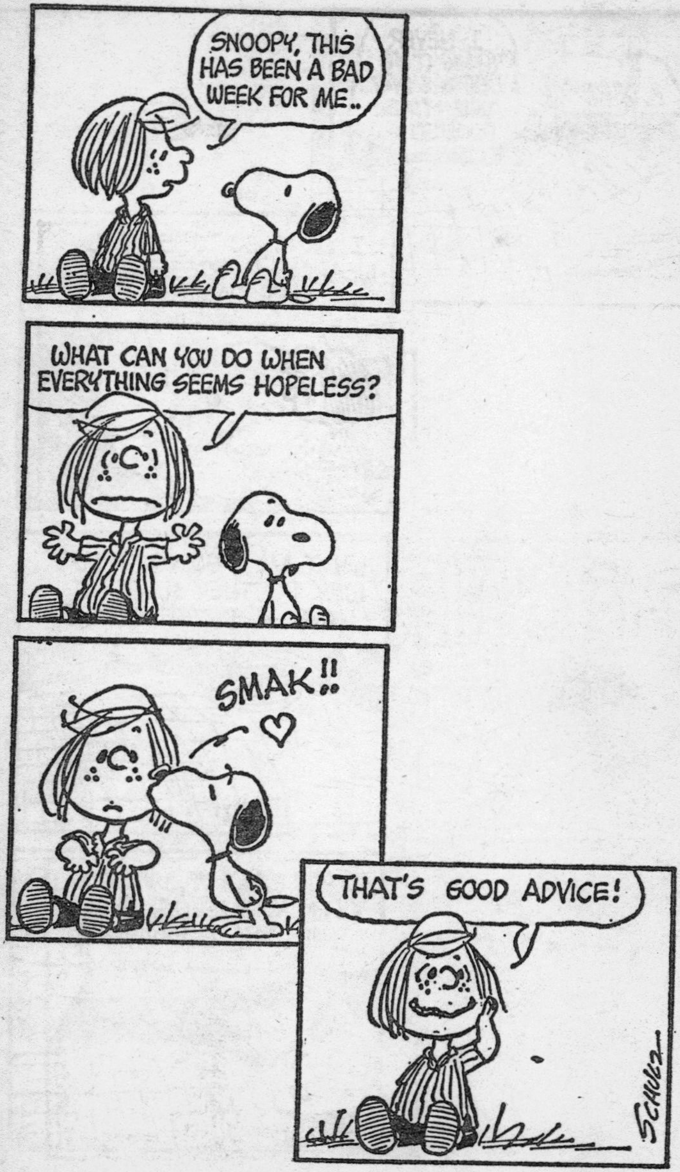
SNOOPY, THIS HAS BEEN A BAD WEEK FOR ME..
WHAT CAN YOU DO WHEN EVERYTHING SEEMS HOPELESS?
SMAK!!
THAT'S GOOD ADVICE!
SCHULZ

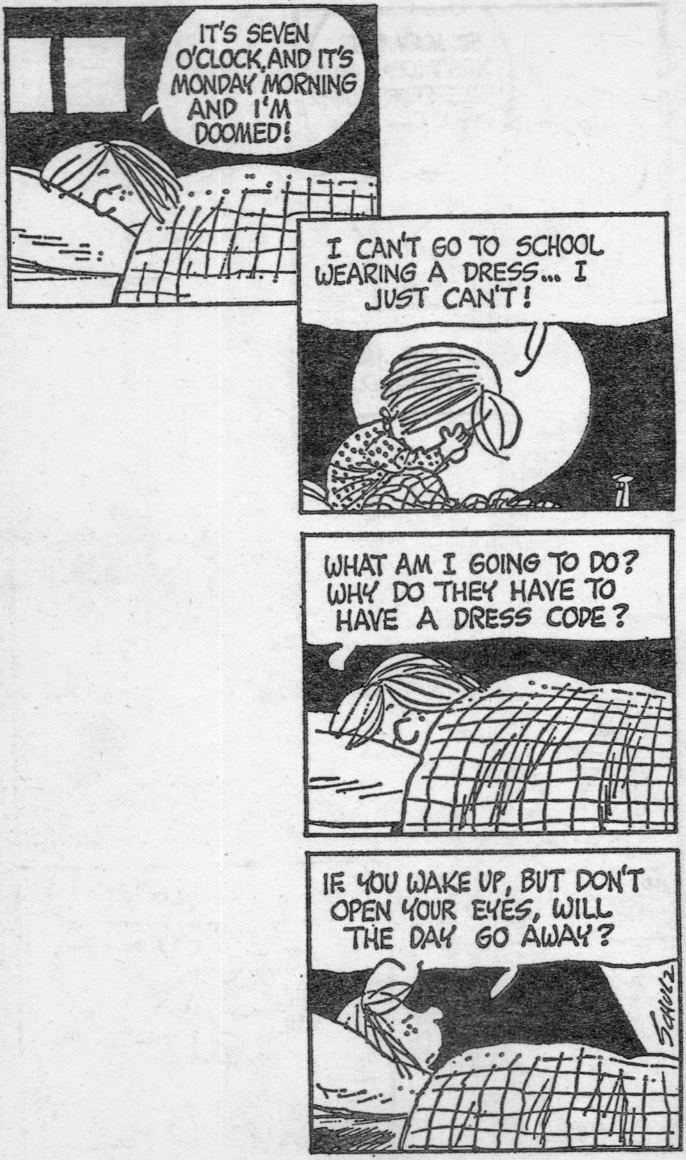
IT'S SEVEN O'CLOCK, AND IT'S MONDAY MORNING AND I'M DOOMED!
I CAN'T GO TO SCHOOL WEARING A DRESS... I JUST CAN'T!
WHAT AM I GOING TO DO? WHY DO THEY HAVE TO HAVE A DRESS CODE?
IF YOU WAKE UP, BUT DON'T OPEN YOUR EYES, WILL THE DAY GO AWAY?
SCHULZ

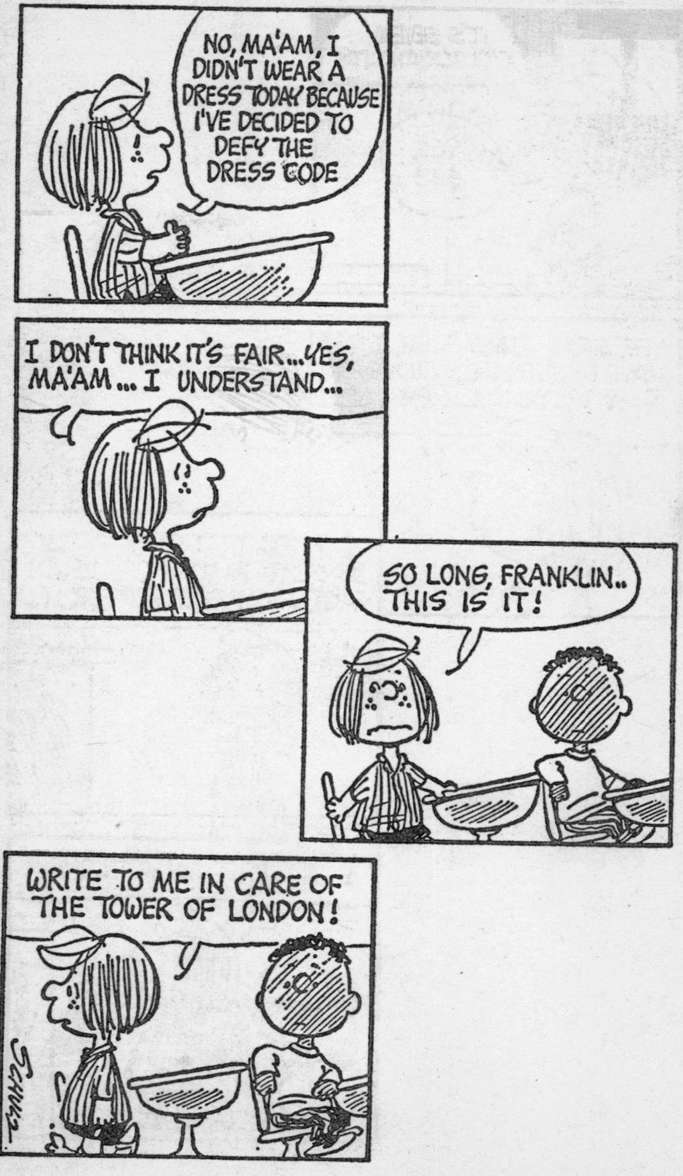
NO, MA'AM, I DIDN'T WEAR A DRESS TODAY BECAUSE I'VE DECIDED TO DEFY THE DRESS CODE
I DON'T THINK IT'S FAIR...YES, MA'AM... I UNDERSTAND...
SO LONG, FRANKLIN.. THIS IS IT!
WRITE TO ME IN CARE OF THE TOWER OF LONDON!
SCHULZ

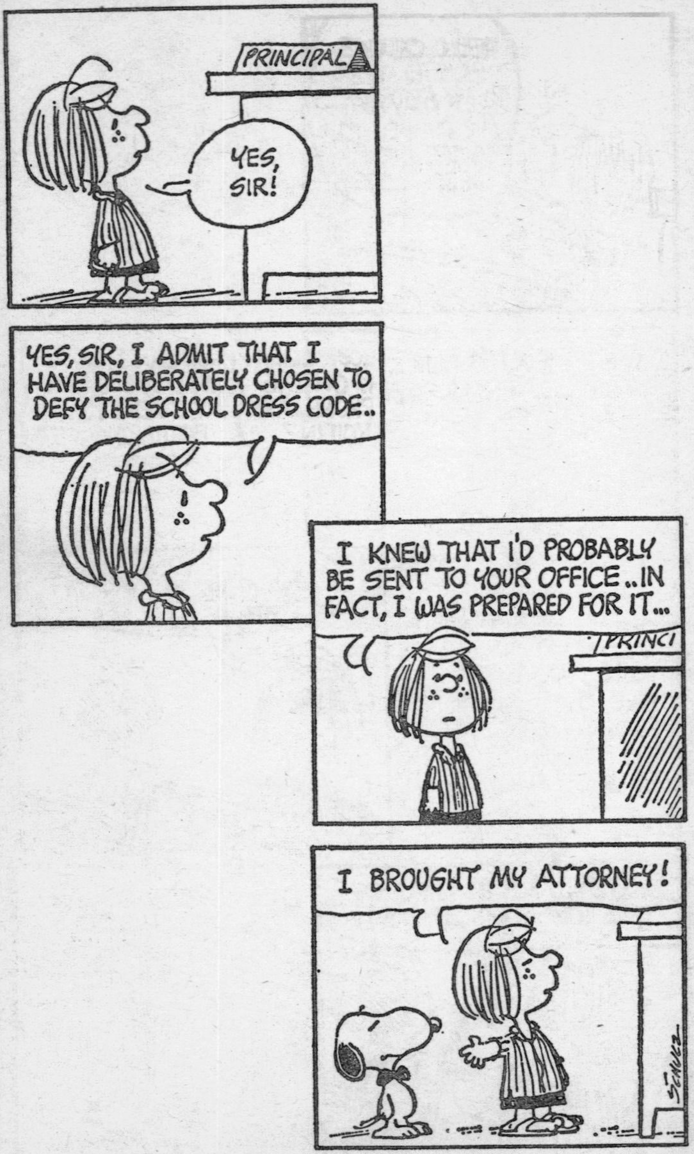
PRINCIPAL
YES, SIR!
YES, SIR, I ADMIT THAT I HAVE DELIBERATELY CHOSEN TO DEFY THE SCHOOL DRESS CODE..
I KNEW THAT I'D PROBABLY BE SENT TO YOUR OFFICE..IN FACT, I WAS PREPARED FOR IT...
PRINCI
I BROUGHT MY ATTORNEY!
SCHULZ

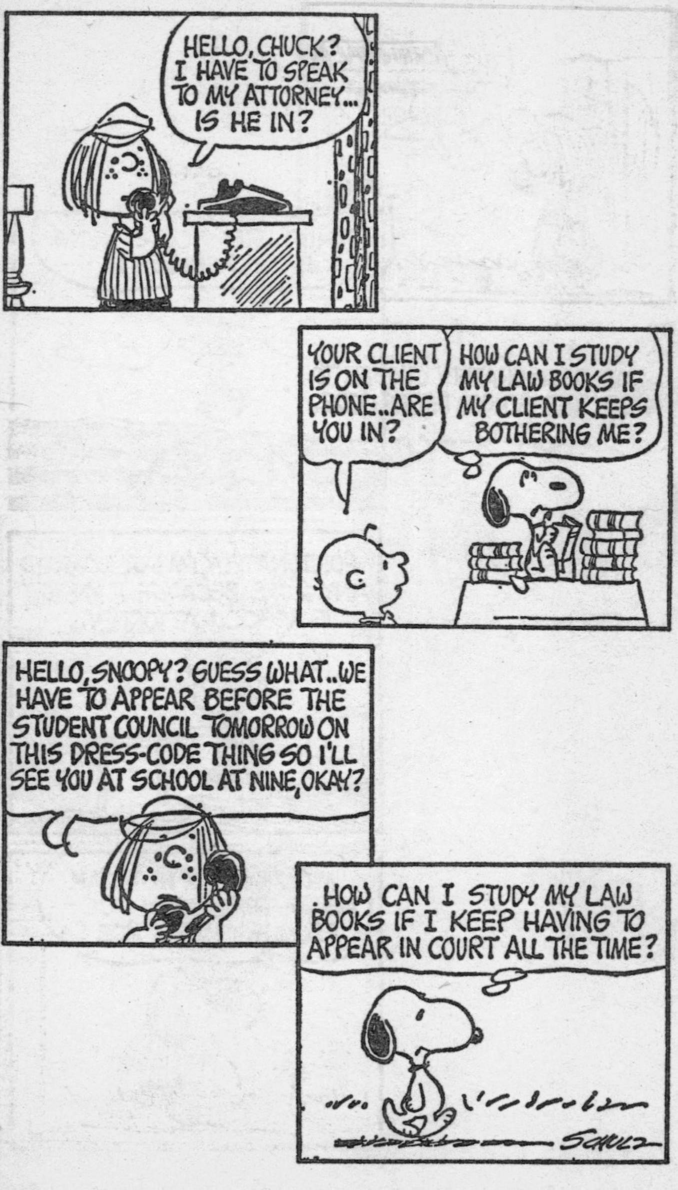
HELLO, CHUCK? I HAVE TO SPEAK TO MY ATTORNEY... IS HE IN?
YOUR CLIENT IS ON THE PHONE..ARE YOU IN?
HOW CAN I STUDY MY LAW BOOKS IF MY CLIENT KEEPS BOTHERING ME?
HELLO, SNOOPY? GUESS WHAT..WE HAVE TO APPEAR BEFORE THE STUDENT COUNCIL TOMORROW ON THIS DRESS-CODE THING SO I'LL SEE YOU AT SCHOOL AT NINE, OKAY?
.HOW CAN I STUDY MY LAW BOOKS IF I KEEP HAVING TO APPEAR IN COURT ALL THE TIME?
SCHULZ

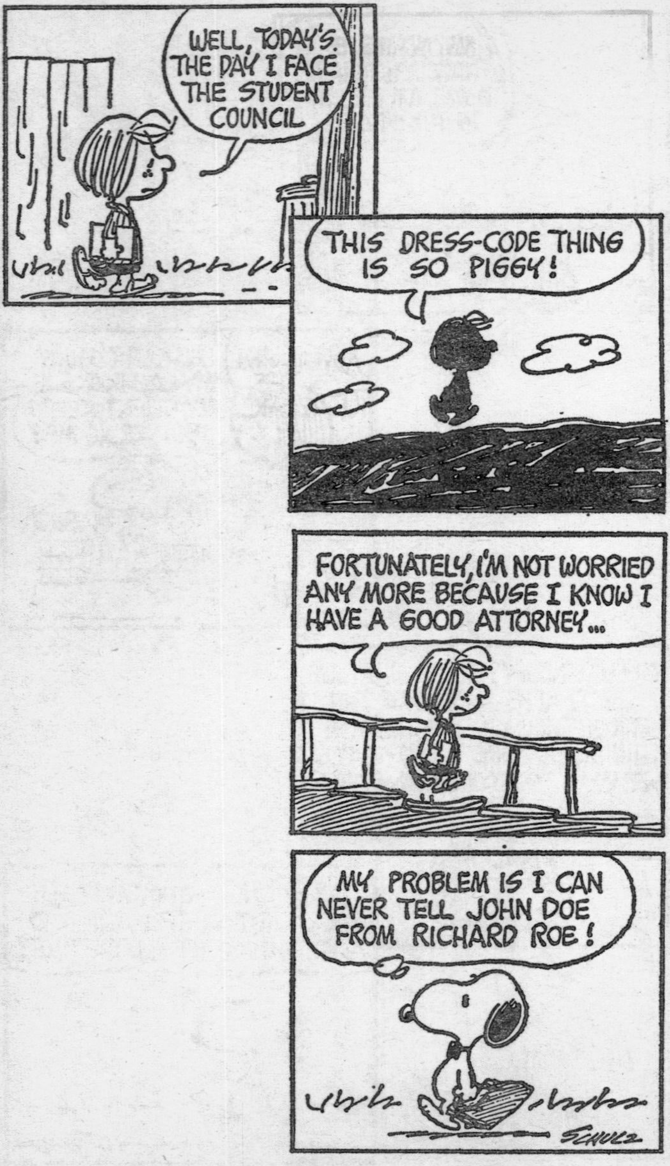
WELL, TODAY'S THE DAY I FACE THE STUDENT COUNCIL
THIS DRESS-CODE THING IS SO PIGGY!
FORTUNATELY, I'M NOT WORRIED ANY MORE BECAUSE I KNOW I HAVE A GOOD ATTORNEY...
MY PROBLEM IS I CAN NEVER TELL JOHN DOE FROM RICHARD ROE!
SCHULZ

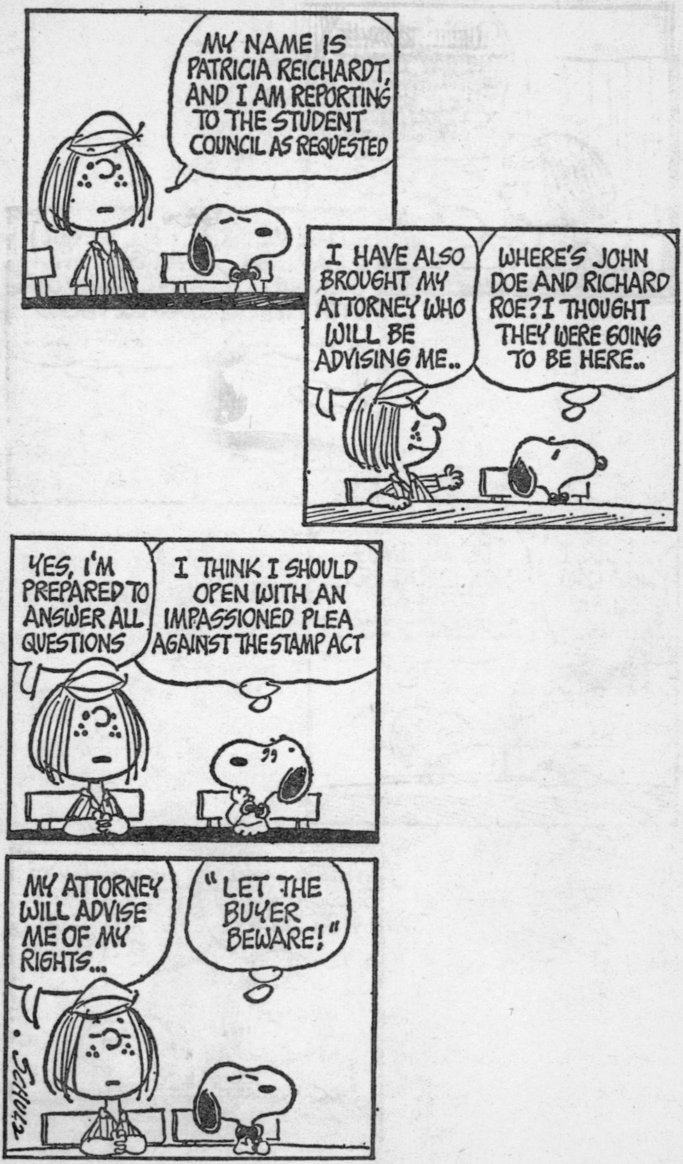
MY NAME IS PATRICIA REICHARDT, AND I AM REPORTING TO THE STUDENT COUNCIL AS REQUESTED
I HAVE ALSO BROUGHT MY ATTORNEY WHO WILL BE ADVISING ME..
WHERE'S JOHN DOE AND RICHARD ROE? I THOUGHT THEY WERE GOING TO BE HERE..
YES, I'M PREPARED TO ANSWER ALL QUESTIONS
I THINK I SHOULD OPEN WITH AN IMPASSIONED PLEA AGAINST THE STAMP ACT
MY ATTORNEY WILL ADVISE ME OF MY RIGHTS...
"LET THE BUYER BEWARE!"
SCHULZ

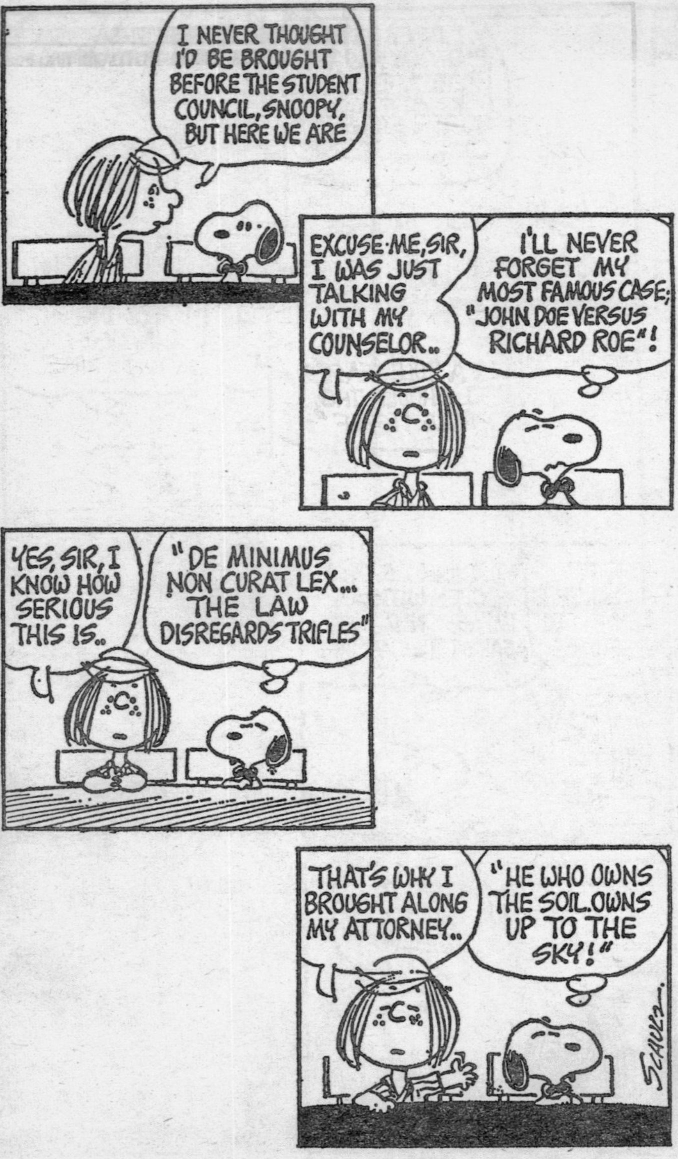
I NEVER THOUGHT I'D BE BROUGHT BEFORE THE STUDENT COUNCIL, SNOOPY, BUT HERE WE ARE
EXCUSE ME, SIR, I WAS JUST TALKING WITH MY COUNSELOR..
I'LL NEVER FORGET MY MOST FAMOUS CASE; "JOHN DOE VERSUS RICHARD ROE"!
YES, SIR, I KNOW HOW SERIOUS THIS IS..
"DE MINIMUS NON CURAT LEX... THE LAW DISREGARDS TRIFLES"
THAT'S WHY I BROUGHT ALONG MY ATTORNEY..
"HE WHO OWNS THE SOIL OWNS UP TO THE SKY!"
SCHULZ

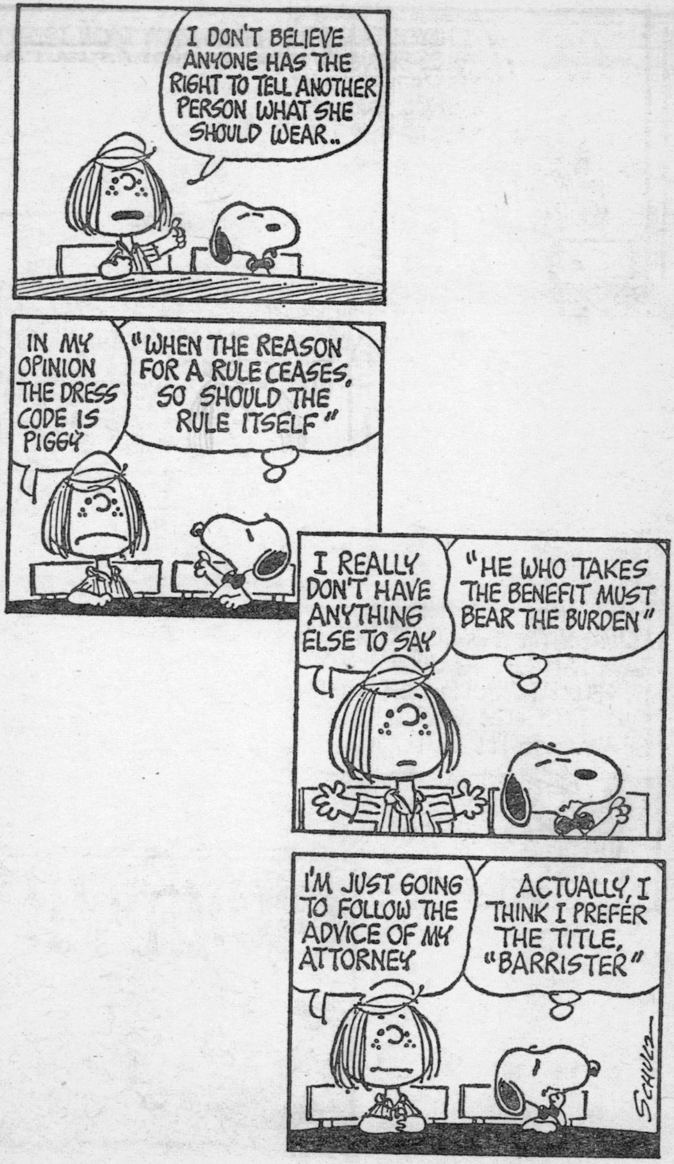

I DON'T BELIEVE ANYONE HAS THE RIGHT TO TELL ANOTHER PERSON WHAT SHE SHOULD WEAR..
IN MY OPINION THE DRESS CODE IS PIGGY
"WHEN THE REASON FOR A RULE CEASES, SO SHOULD THE RULE ITSELF"
I REALLY DON'T HAVE ANYTHING ELSE TO SAY
"HE WHO TAKES THE BENEFIT MUST BEAR THE BURDEN"
I'M JUST GOING TO FOLLOW THE ADVICE OF MY ATTORNEY
ACTUALLY, I THINK I PREFER THE TITLE, "BARRISTER"
SCHULZ

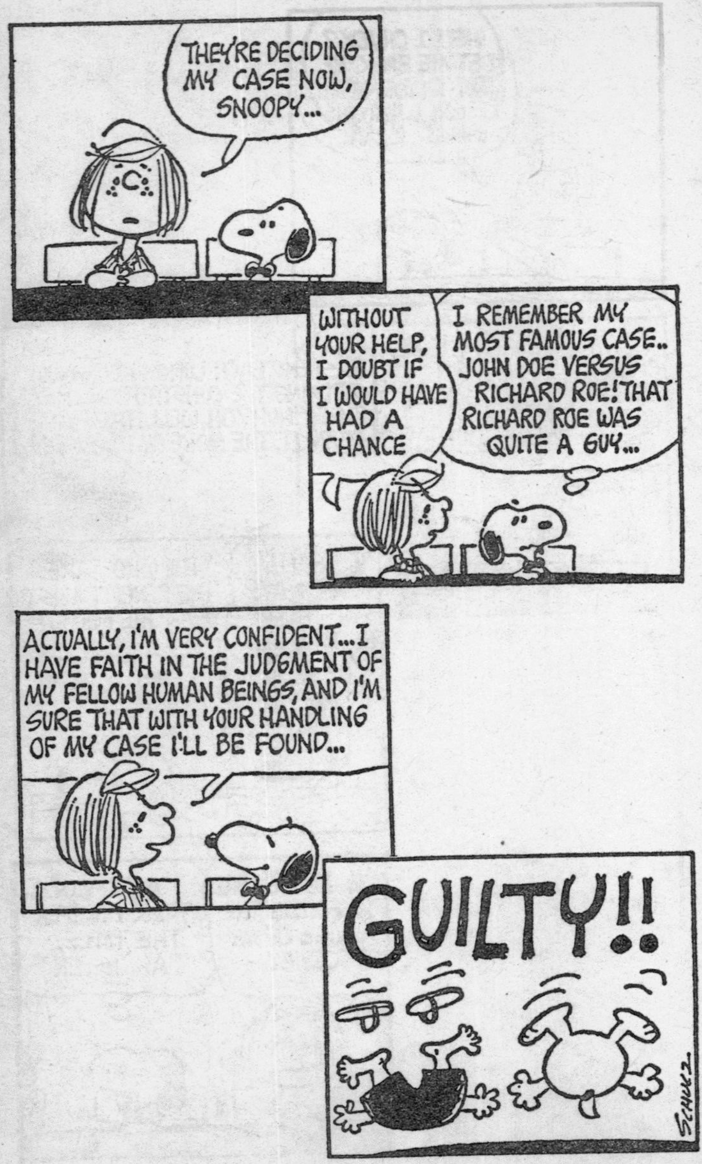
THEY'RE DECIDING MY CASE NOW, SNOOPY...
WITHOUT YOUR HELP, I DOUBT IF I WOULD HAVE HAD A CHANCE
I REMEMBER MY MOST FAMOUS CASE.. JOHN DOE VERSUS RICHARD ROE! THAT RICHARD ROE WAS QUITE A GUY...
ACTUALLY, I'M VERY CONFIDENT...I HAVE FAITH IN THE JUDGMENT OF MY FELLOW HUMAN BEINGS, AND I'M SURE THAT WITH YOUR HANDLING OF MY CASE I'LL BE FOUND...
GUILTY!!
SCHULZ

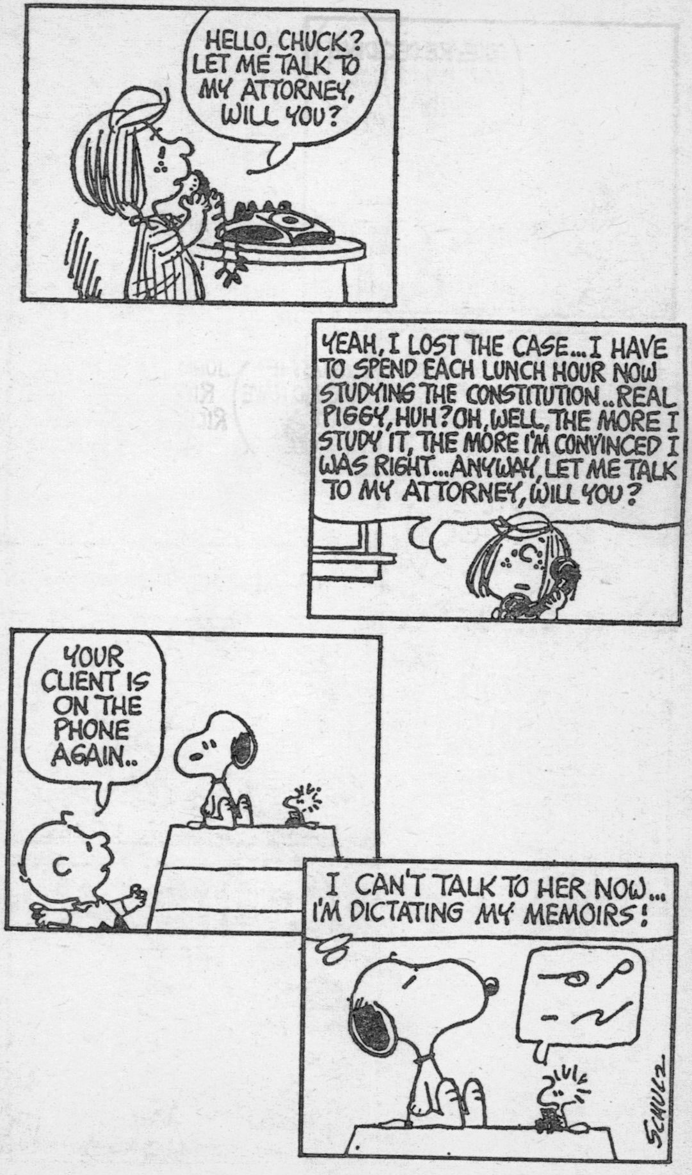

HELLO, CHUCK? LET ME TALK TO MY ATTORNEY, WILL YOU?
YEAH, I LOST THE CASE...I HAVE TO SPEND EACH LUNCH HOUR NOW STUDYING THE CONSTITUTION..REAL PIGGY, HUH? OH, WELL, THE MORE I STUDY IT, THE MORE I'M CONVINCED I WAS RIGHT...ANYWAY, LET ME TALK TO MY ATTORNEY, WILL YOU?
YOUR CLIENT IS ON THE PHONE AGAIN..
I CAN'T TALK TO HER NOW... I'M DICTATING MY MEMOIRS!
SCHULZ

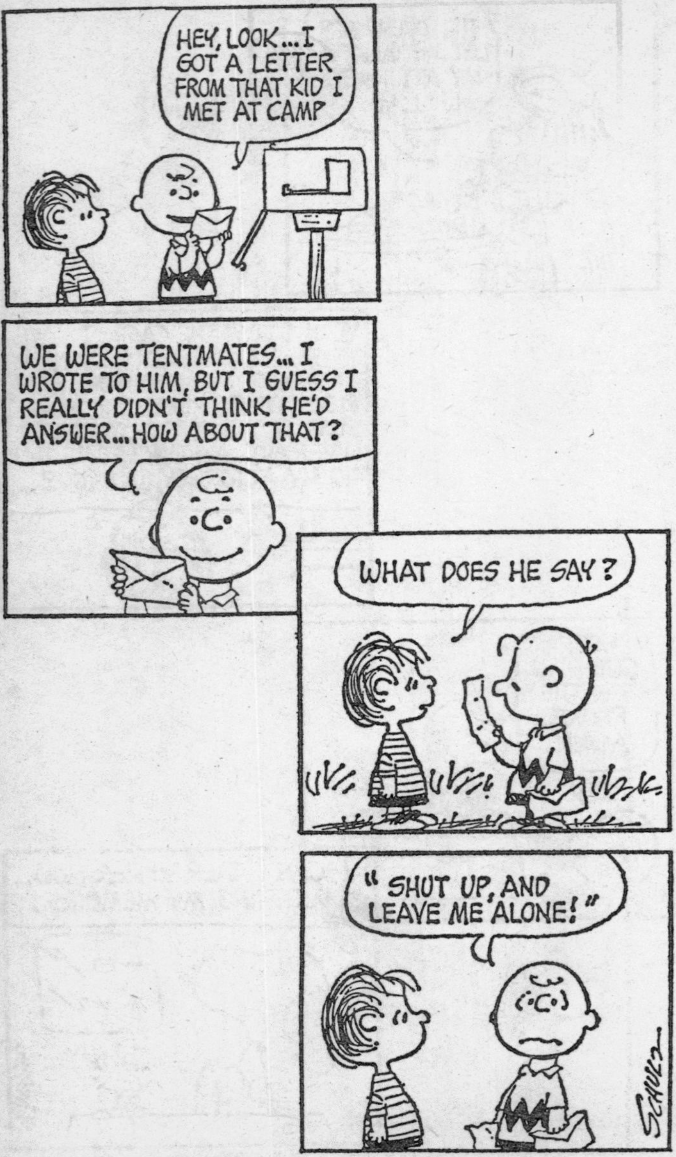
HEY, LOOK...I GOT A LETTER FROM THAT KID I MET AT CAMP
WE WERE TENTMATES... I WROTE TO HIM, BUT I GUESS I REALLY DIDN'T THINK HE'D ANSWER...HOW ABOUT THAT?
WHAT DOES HE SAY?
"SHUT UP, AND LEAVE ME ALONE!"
SCHULZ

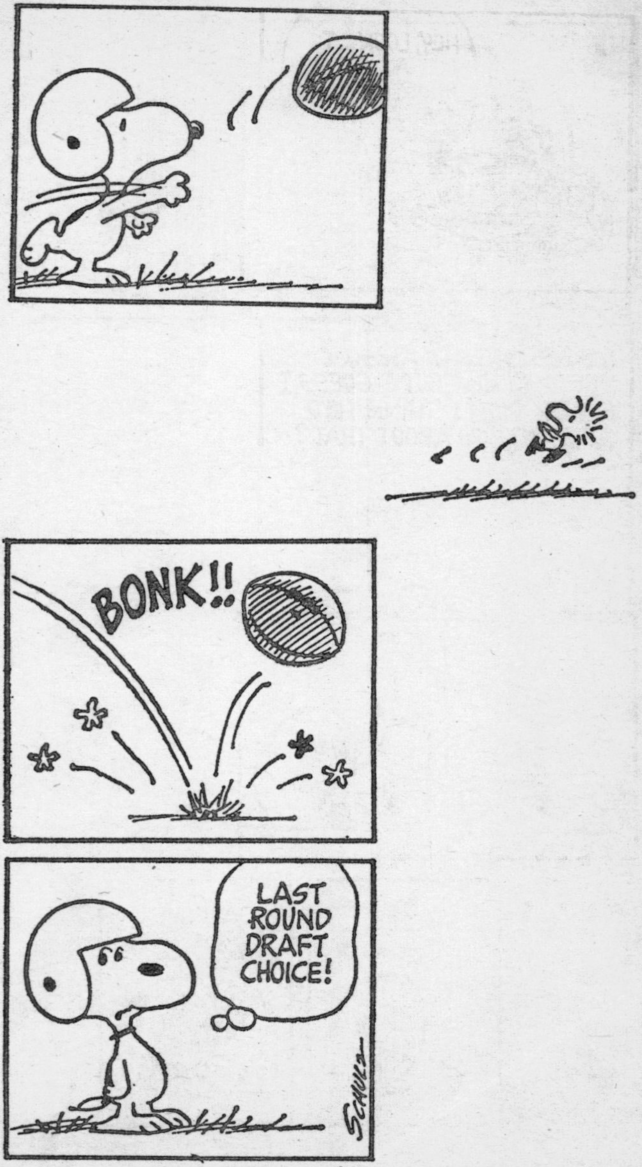
BONK!!
LAST ROUND DRAFT CHOICE!
SCHULZ

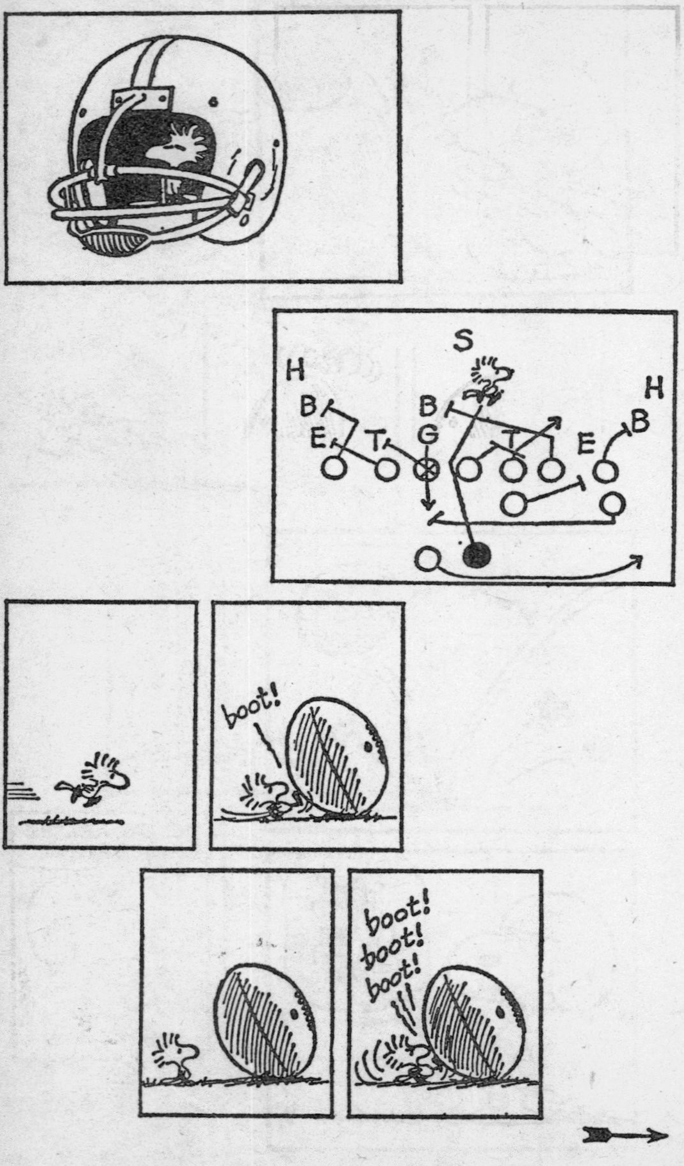
S
H
B
E
T
B
G
T
H
B
E
boot!
boot!
boot!
boot!

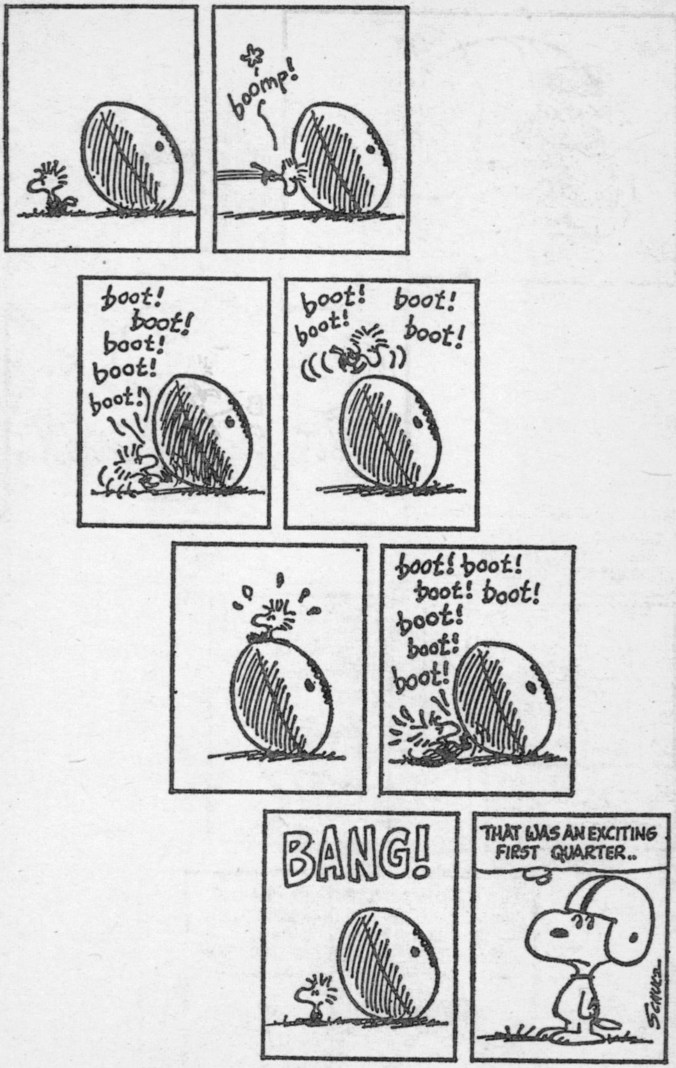
boomp!
boot! boot! boot! boot! boot!
boot! boot! boot! boot!
boot! boot! boot! boot! boot! boot! boot!
BANG!
THAT WAS AN EXCITING FIRST QUARTER..
SCHULZ

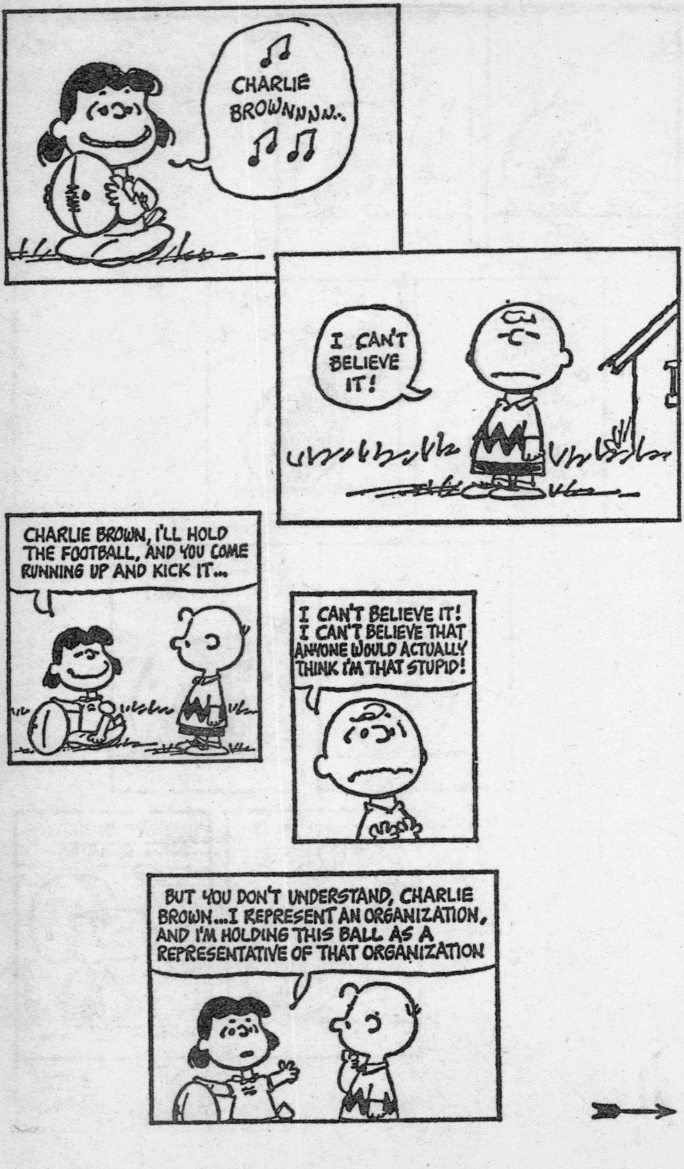
CHARLIE BROWNNNNN..
I CAN'T BELIEVE IT!
CHARLIE BROWN, I'LL HOLD THE FOOTBALL, AND YOU COME RUNNING UP AND KICK IT...
I CAN'T BELIEVE IT! I CAN'T BELIEVE THAT ANYONE WOULD ACTUALLY THINK I'M THAT STUPID!
BUT YOU DON'T UNDERSTAND, CHARLIE BROWN...I REPRESENT AN ORGANIZATION, AND I'M HOLDING THIS BALL AS A REPRESENTATIVE OF THAT ORGANIZATION

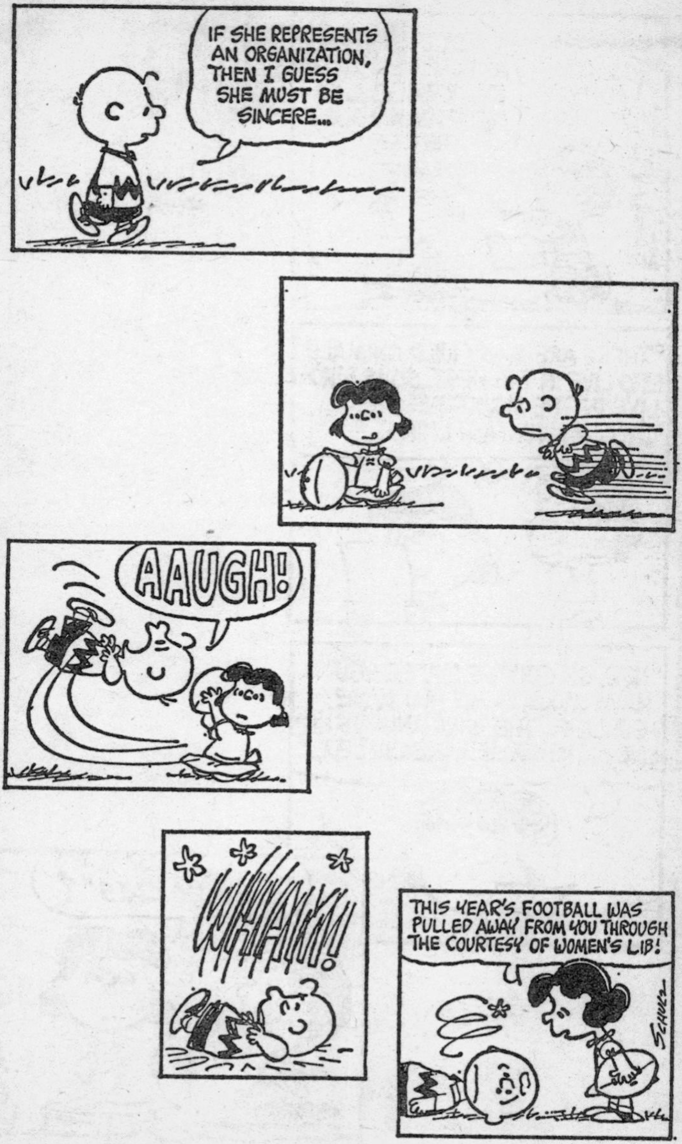
IF SHE REPRESENTS AN ORGANIZATION, THEN I GUESS SHE MUST BE SINCERE...
AAUGH!
WHAM!
THIS YEAR'S FOOTBALL WAS PULLED AWAY FROM YOU THROUGH THE COURTESY OF WOMEN'S LIB!
SCHULZ

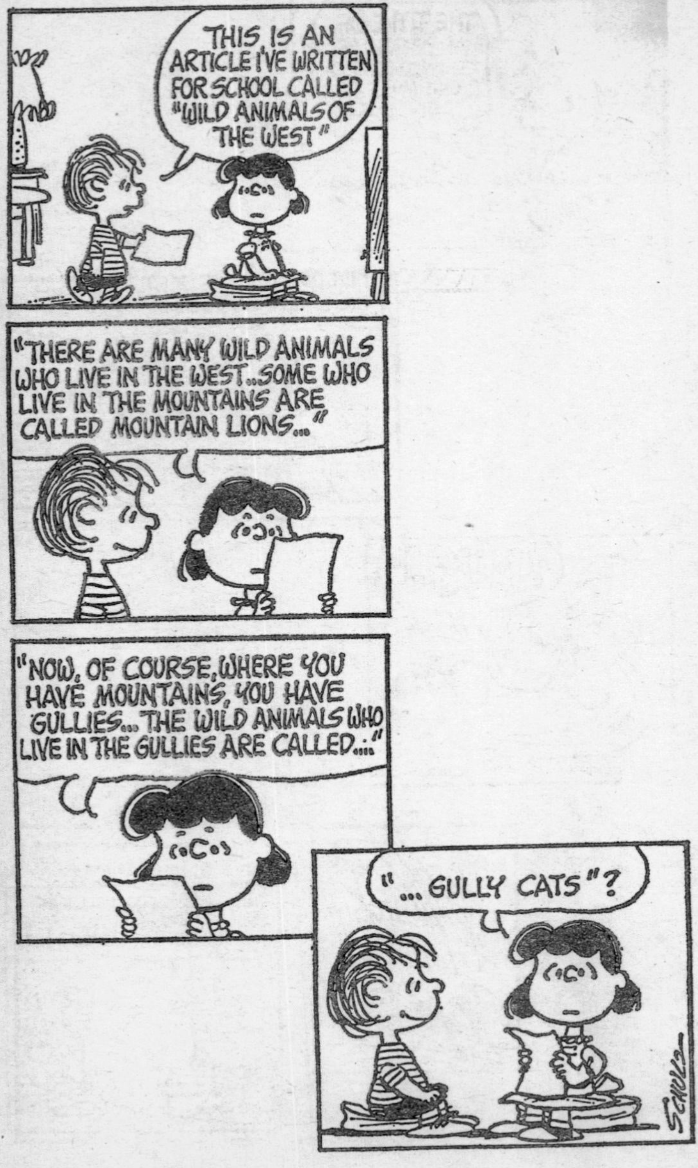
THIS IS AN ARTICLE I'VE WRITTEN FOR SCHOOL CALLED "WILD ANIMALS OF THE WEST"
"THERE ARE MANY WILD ANIMALS WHO LIVE IN THE WEST..SOME WHO LIVE IN THE MOUNTAINS ARE CALLED MOUNTAIN LIONS..."
"NOW, OF COURSE, WHERE YOU HAVE MOUNTAINS, YOU HAVE GULLIES... THE WILD ANIMALS WHO LIVE IN THE GULLIES ARE CALLED...."
"... GULLY CATS"?
SCHULZ

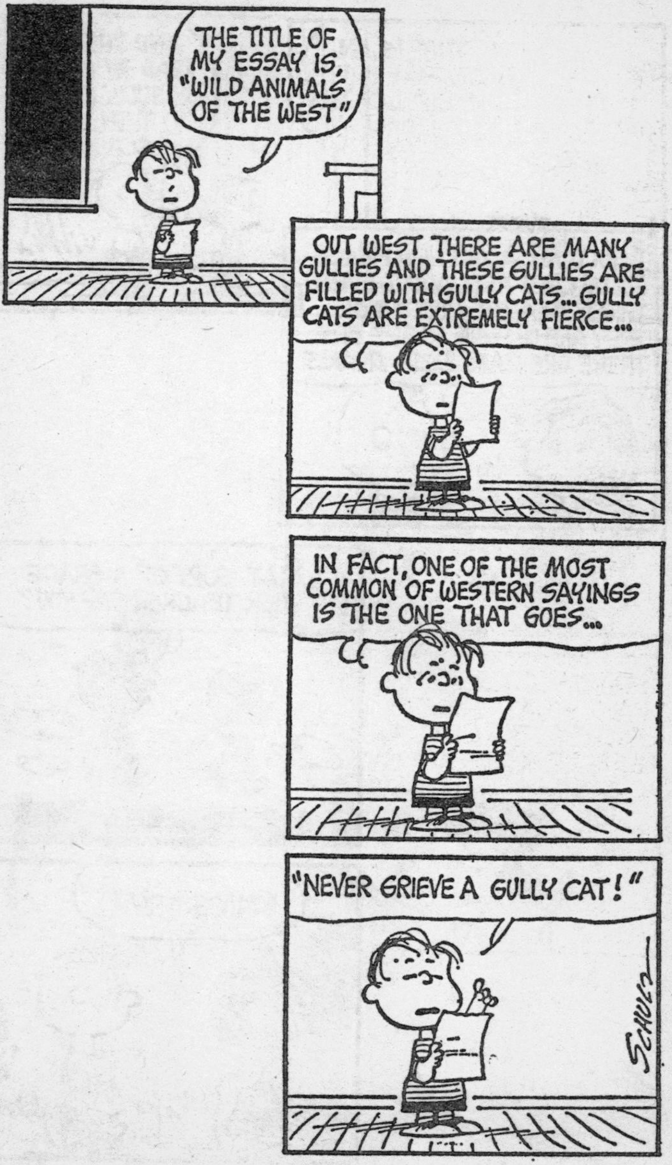
THE TITLE OF MY ESSAY IS, "WILD ANIMALS OF THE WEST"
OUT WEST THERE ARE MANY GULLIES AND THESE GULLIES ARE FILLED WITH GULLY CATS... GULLY CATS ARE EXTREMELY FIERCE...
IN FACT, ONE OF THE MOST COMMON OF WESTERN SAYINGS IS THE ONE THAT GOES...
"NEVER GRIEVE A GULLY CAT!"
SCHULZ

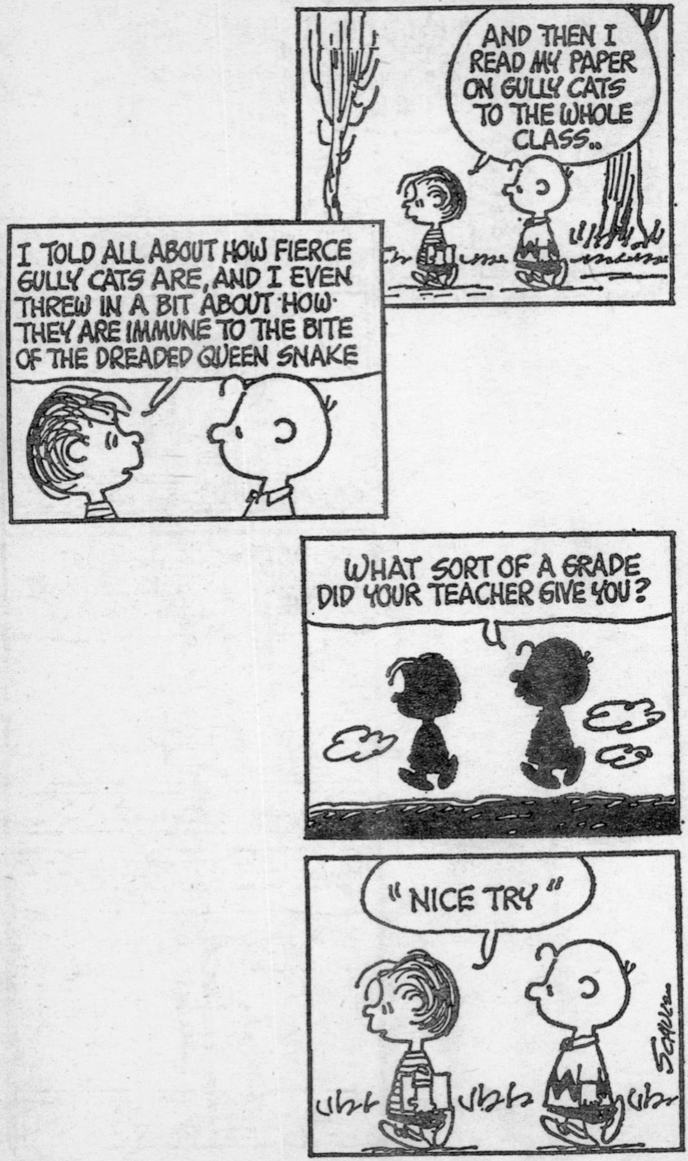
AND THEN I READ MY PAPER ON GULLY CATS TO THE WHOLE CLASS..
I TOLD ALL ABOUT HOW FIERCE GULLY CATS ARE, AND I EVEN THREW IN A BIT ABOUT HOW THEY ARE IMMUNE TO THE BITE OF THE DREADED QUEEN SNAKE
WHAT SORT OF A GRADE DID YOUR TEACHER GIVE YOU?
"NICE TRY"
SCHULZ

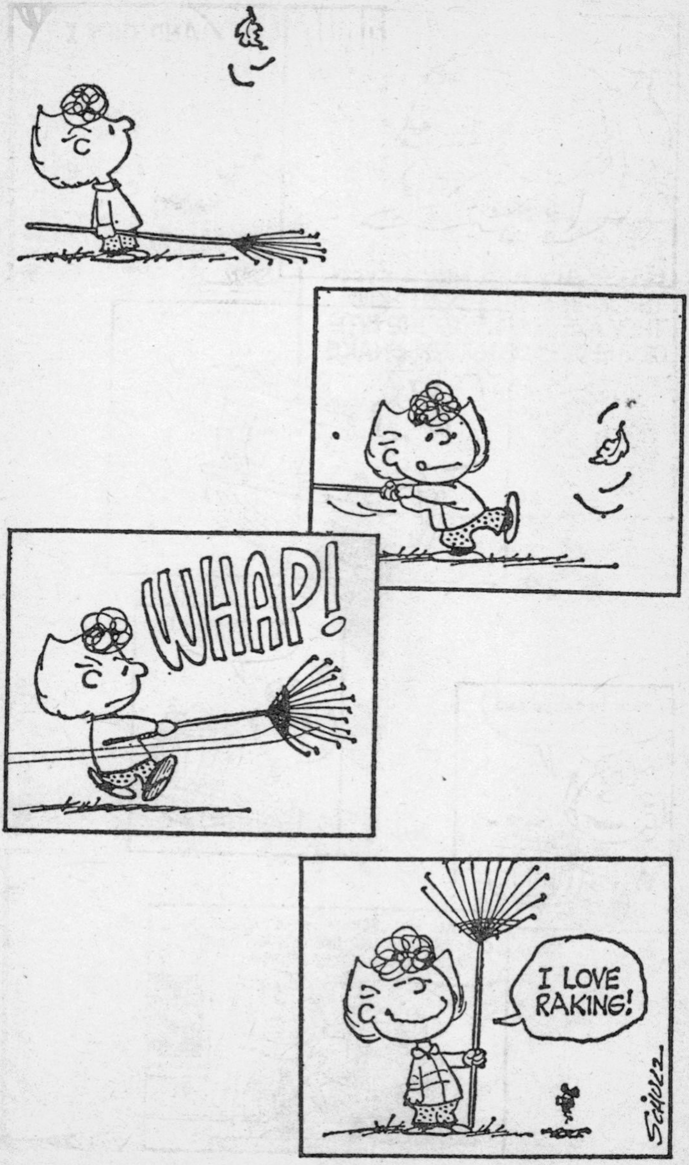
WHAP!
I LOVE RAKING!
SCHULZ

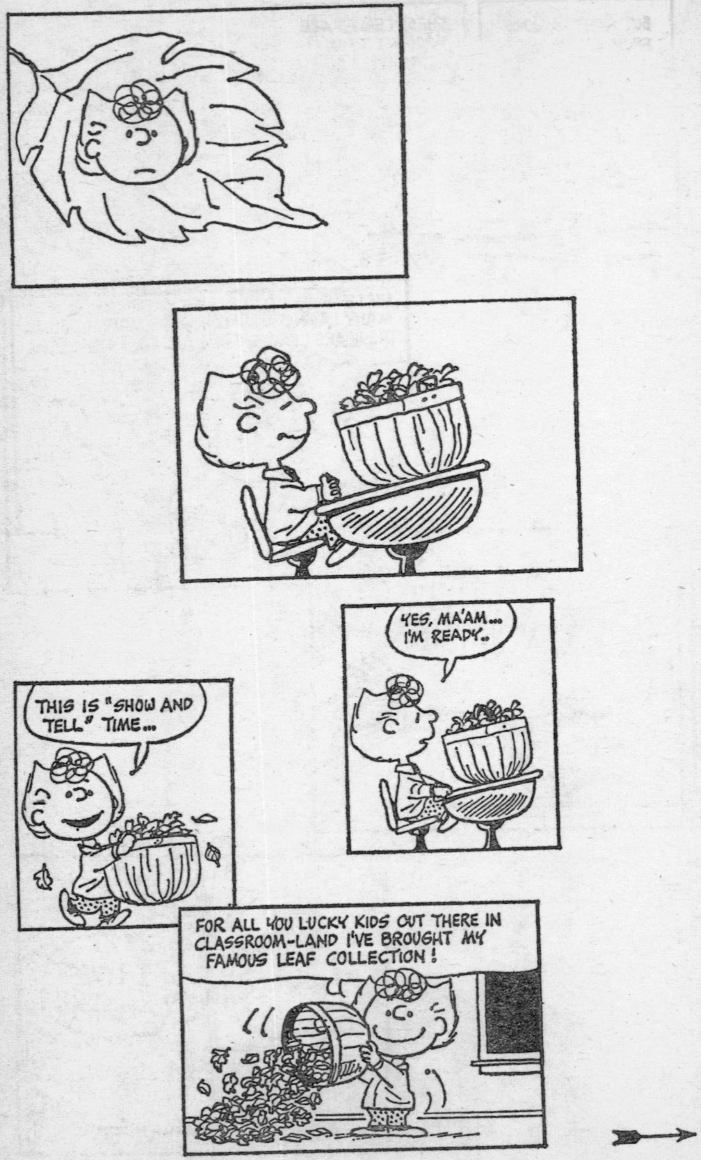
YES, MA'AM... I'M READY..
THIS IS "SHOW AND TELL" TIME...
FOR ALL YOU LUCKY KIDS OUT THERE IN CLASSROOM-LAND I'VE BROUGHT MY FAMOUS LEAF COLLECTION!

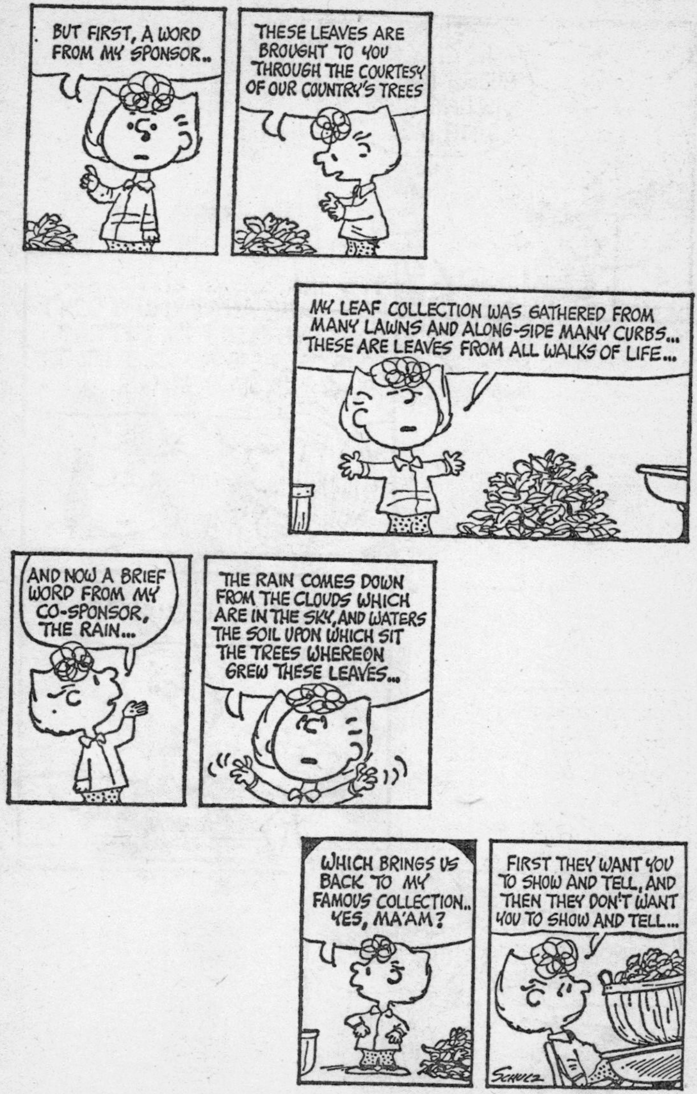
BUT FIRST, A WORD FROM MY SPONSOR..
THESE LEAVES ARE BROUGHT TO YOU THROUGH THE COURTESY OF OUR COUNTRY'S TREES
MY LEAF COLLECTION WAS GATHERED FROM MANY LAWNS AND ALONG-SIDE MANY CURBS... THESE ARE LEAVES FROM ALL WALKS OF LIFE...
AND NOW A BRIEF WORD FROM MY CO-SPONSOR, THE RAIN...
THE RAIN COMES DOWN FROM THE CLOUDS WHICH ARE IN THE SKY, AND WATERS THE SOIL UPON WHICH SIT THE TREES WHEREON GREW THESE LEAVES...
WHICH BRINGS US BACK TO MY FAMOUS COLLECTION.. YES, MA'AM?
FIRST THEY WANT YOU TO SHOW AND TELL, AND THEN THEY DON'T WANT YOU TO SHOW AND TELL...
SCHULZ

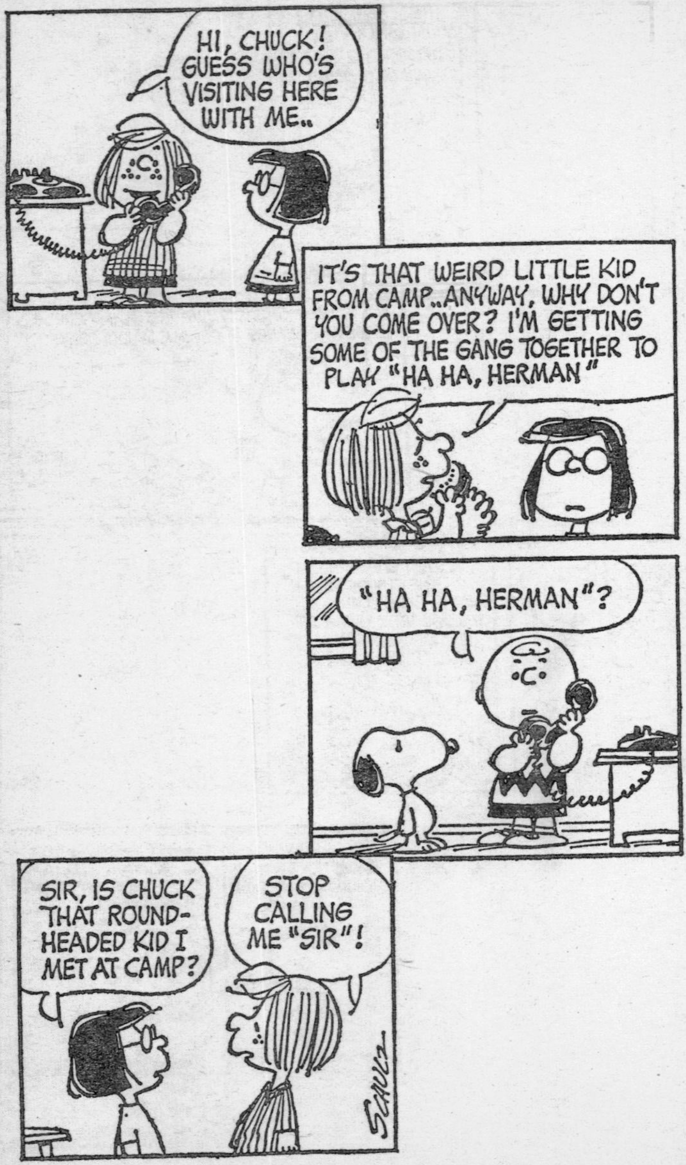
HI, CHUCK! GUESS WHO'S VISITING HERE WITH ME..
IT'S THAT WEIRD LITTLE KID FROM CAMP..ANYWAY, WHY DON'T YOU COME OVER? I'M GETTING SOME OF THE GANG TOGETHER TO PLAY "HA HA, HERMAN"
"HA HA, HERMAN"?
SIR, IS CHUCK THAT ROUND-HEADED KID I MET AT CAMP?
STOP CALLING ME "SIR"!
SCHULZ

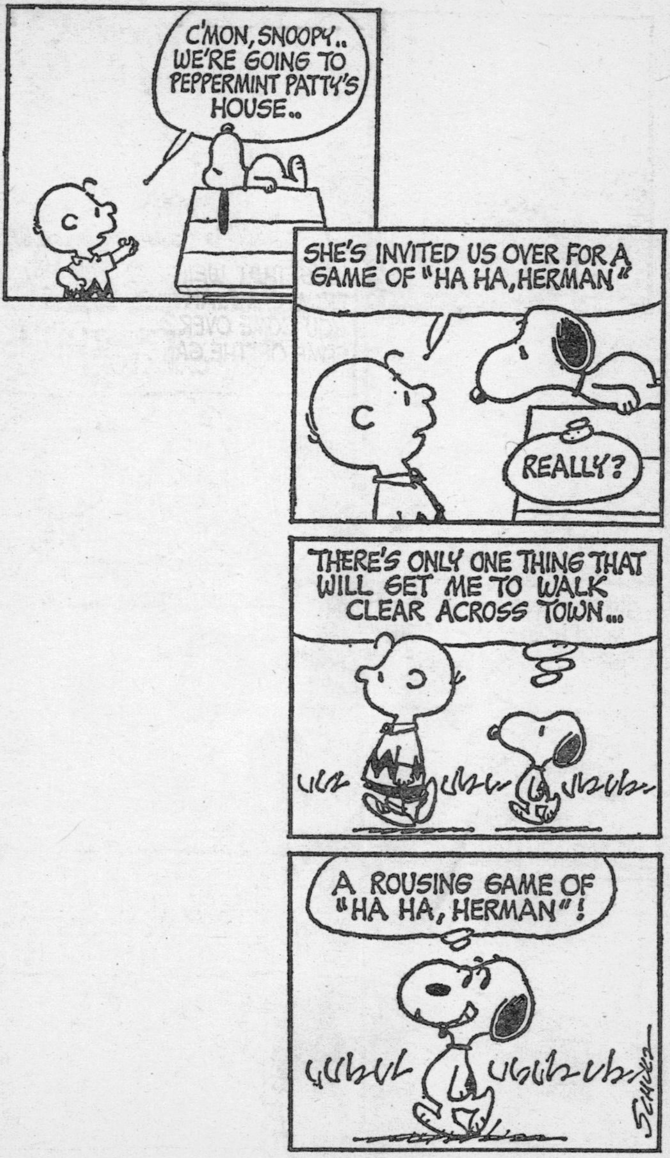
C'MON, SNOOPY..
WE'RE GOING TO
PEPPERMINT PATTY'S
HOUSE..
SHE'S INVITED US OVER FOR A
GAME OF "HA HA, HERMAN"
REALLY?
THERE'S ONLY ONE THING THAT
WILL GET ME TO WALK
CLEAR ACROSS TOWN...
A ROUSING GAME OF
"HA HA, HERMAN"!
SCHULZ

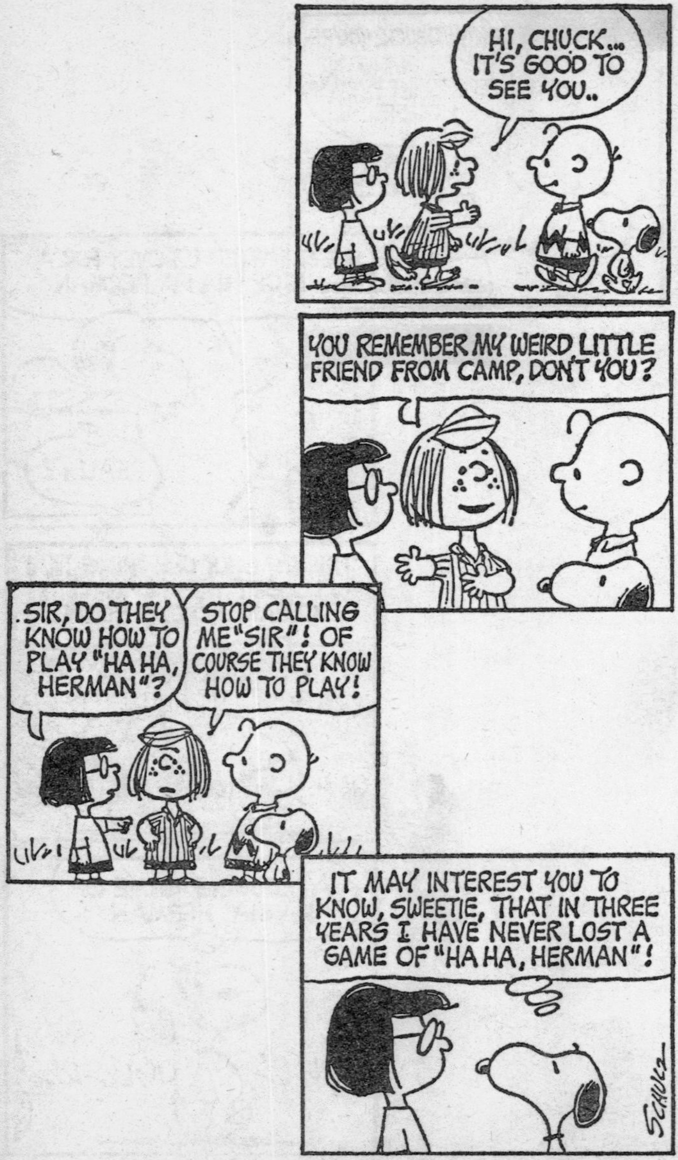
HI, CHUCK... IT'S GOOD TO SEE YOU..
YOU REMEMBER MY WEIRD LITTLE FRIEND FROM CAMP, DON'T YOU?
SIR, DO THEY KNOW HOW TO PLAY "HA HA, HERMAN"?
STOP CALLING ME "SIR"! OF COURSE THEY KNOW HOW TO PLAY!
IT MAY INTEREST YOU TO KNOW, SWEETIE, THAT IN THREE YEARS I HAVE NEVER LOST A GAME OF "HA HA, HERMAN"!
SCHULZ

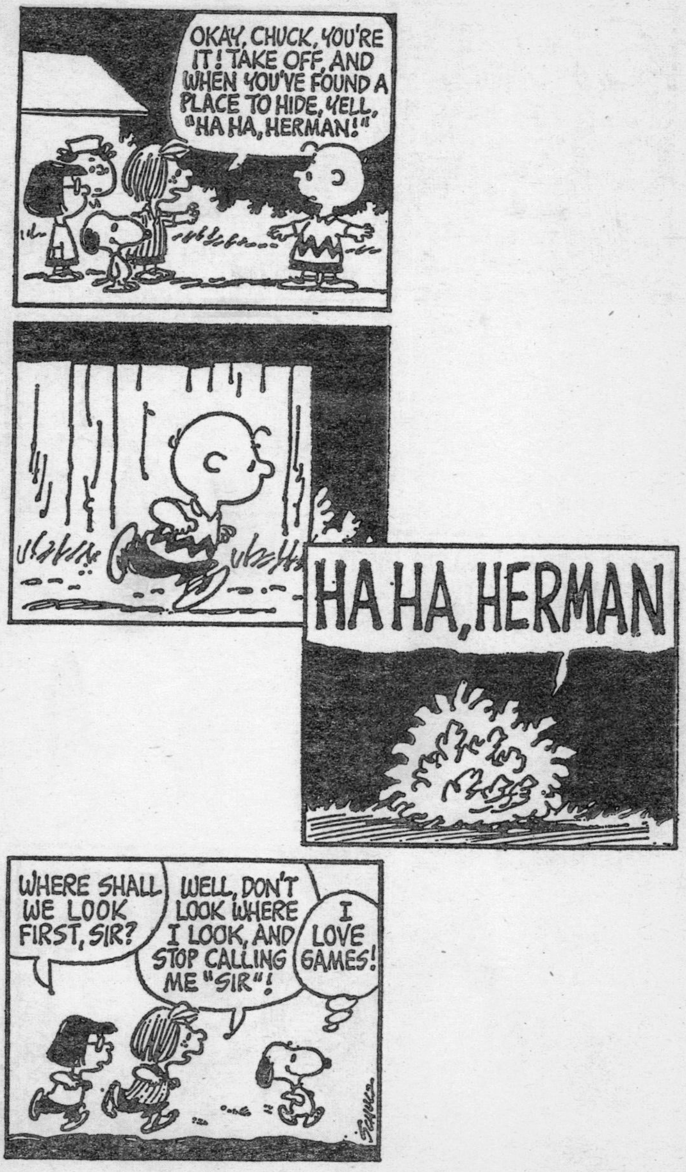
OKAY, CHUCK, YOU'RE IT! TAKE OFF, AND WHEN YOU'VE FOUND A PLACE TO HIDE, YELL, "HA HA, HERMAN!"
HA HA, HERMAN
WHERE SHALL WE LOOK FIRST, SIR?
WELL, DON'T LOOK WHERE I LOOK, AND STOP CALLING ME "SIR"!
I LOVE GAMES!

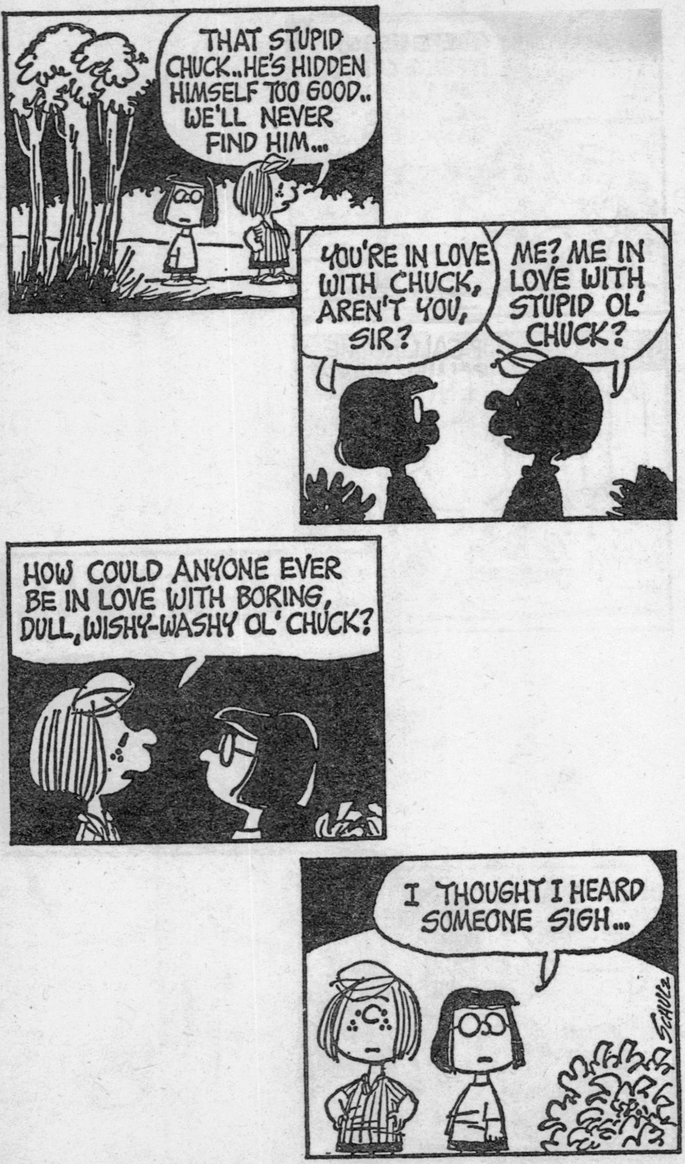
THAT STUPID CHUCK..HE'S HIDDEN HIMSELF TOO GOOD.. WE'LL NEVER FIND HIM...
YOU'RE IN LOVE WITH CHUCK, AREN'T YOU, SIR?
ME? ME IN LOVE WITH STUPID OL' CHUCK?
HOW COULD ANYONE EVER BE IN LOVE WITH BORING, DULL, WISHY-WASHY OL' CHUCK?
I THOUGHT I HEARD SOMEONE SIGH...
SCHULZ

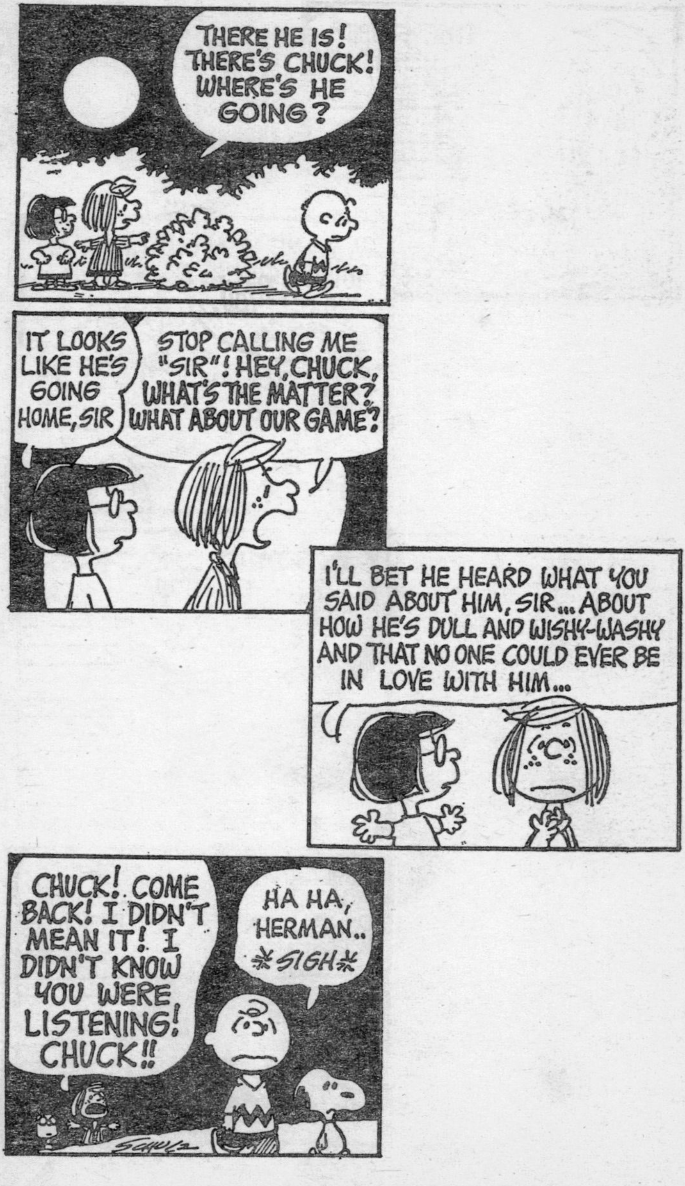
THERE HE IS! THERE'S CHUCK! WHERE'S HE GOING?
IT LOOKS LIKE HE'S GOING HOME, SIR
STOP CALLING ME "SIR"! HEY, CHUCK, WHAT'S THE MATTER? WHAT ABOUT OUR GAME?
I'LL BET HE HEARD WHAT YOU SAID ABOUT HIM, SIR... ABOUT HOW HE'S DULL AND WISHY-WASHY AND THAT NO ONE COULD EVER BE IN LOVE WITH HIM...
CHUCK! COME BACK! I DIDN'T MEAN IT! I DIDN'T KNOW YOU WERE LISTENING! CHUCK!!
HA HA, HERMAN.. *SIGH*

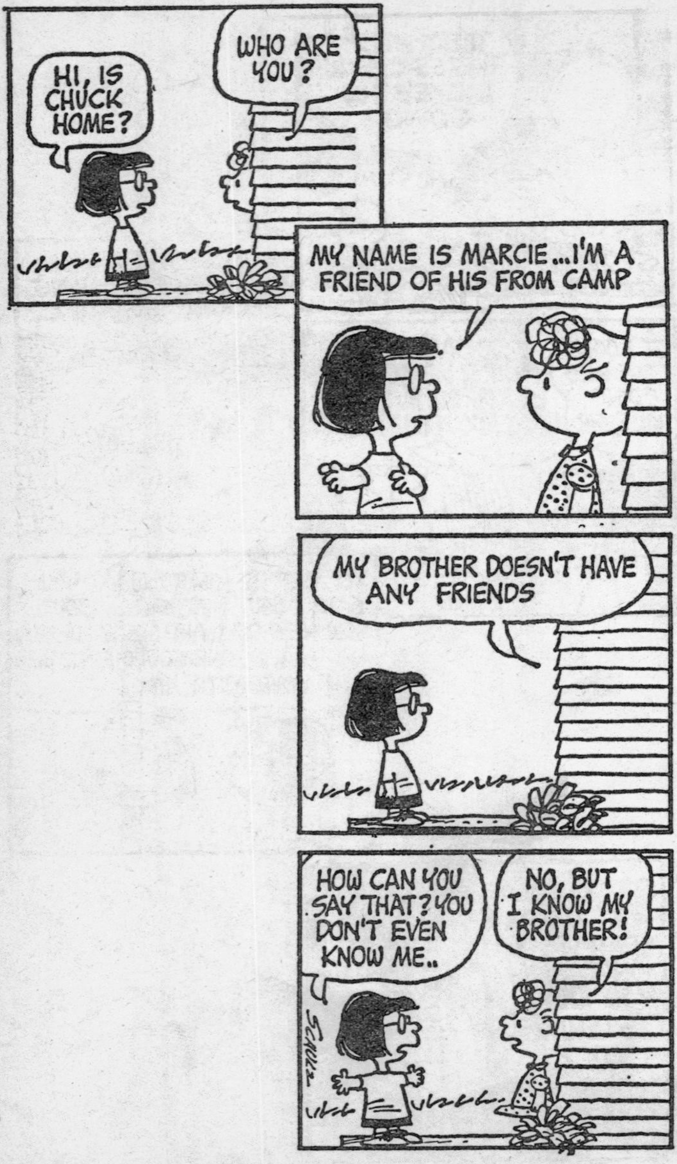
HI, IS CHUCK HOME?
WHO ARE YOU?
MY NAME IS MARCIE...I'M A FRIEND OF HIS FROM CAMP
MY BROTHER DOESN'T HAVE ANY FRIENDS
HOW CAN YOU SAY THAT? YOU DON'T EVEN KNOW ME..
NO, BUT I KNOW MY BROTHER!
SCHULZ

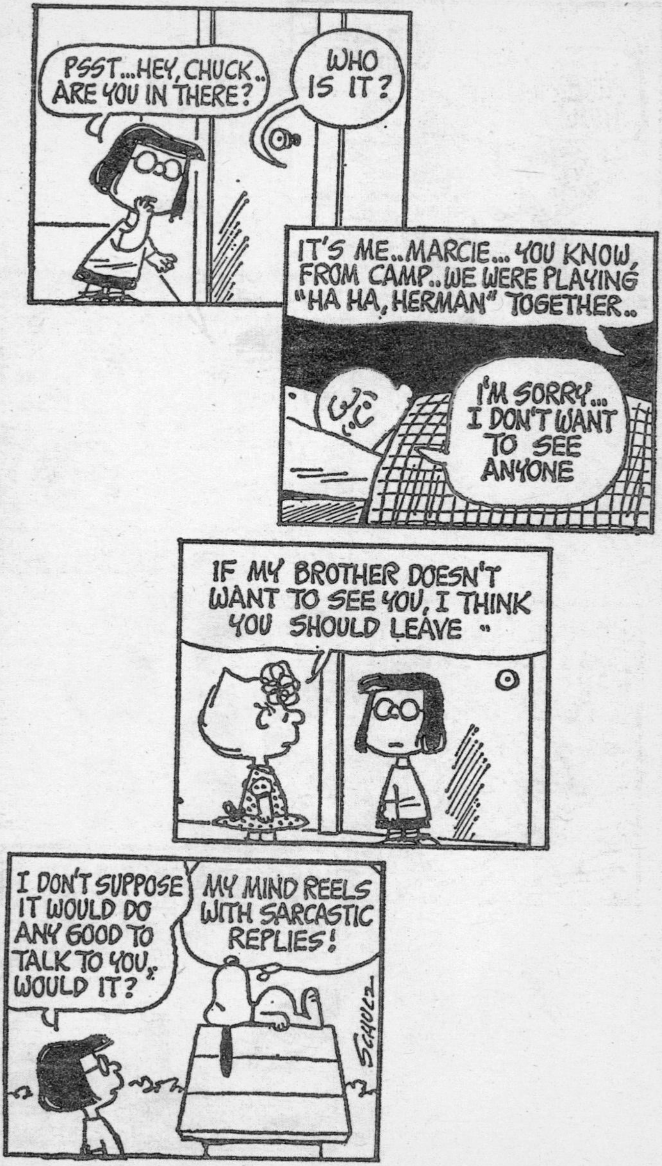
PSST...HEY, CHUCK.. ARE YOU IN THERE?
WHO IS IT?
IT'S ME..MARCIE... YOU KNOW, FROM CAMP..WE WERE PLAYING "HA HA, HERMAN" TOGETHER..
I'M SORRY... I DON'T WANT TO SEE ANYONE
IF MY BROTHER DOESN'T WANT TO SEE YOU, I THINK YOU SHOULD LEAVE
I DON'T SUPPOSE IT WOULD DO ANY GOOD TO TALK TO YOU, WOULD IT?
MY MIND REELS WITH SARCASTIC REPLIES!
SCHULZ

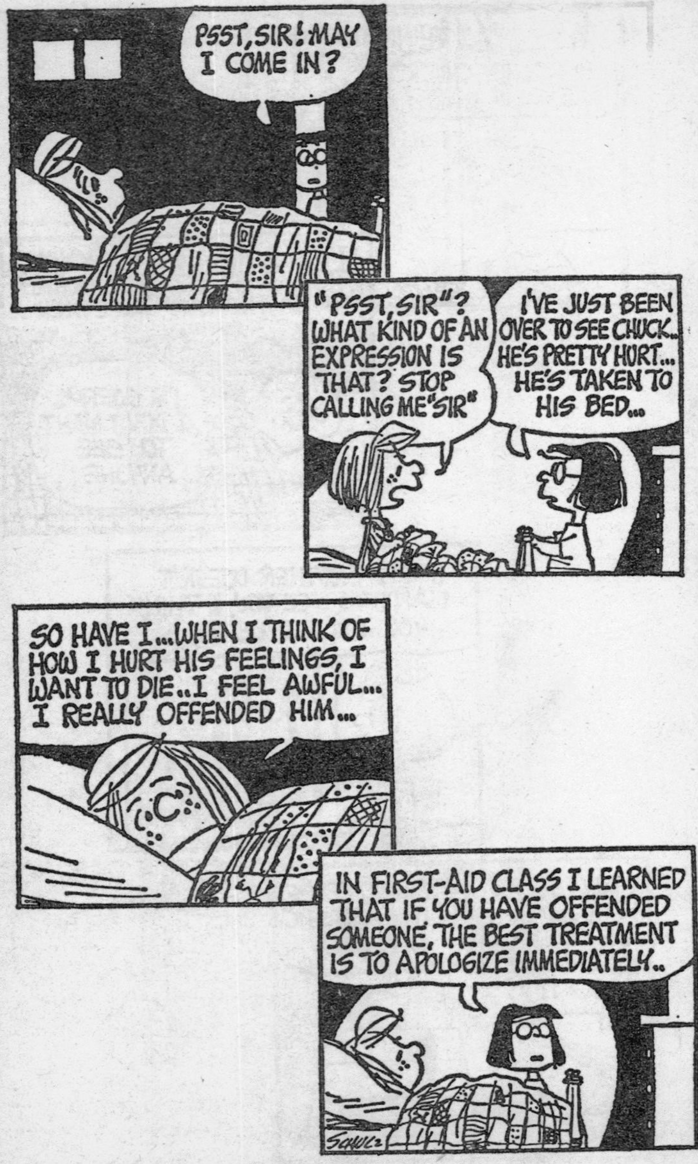
PSST, SIR! MAY I COME IN?
"PSST, SIR"? WHAT KIND OF AN EXPRESSION IS THAT? STOP CALLING ME "SIR"
I'VE JUST BEEN OVER TO SEE CHUCK.. HE'S PRETTY HURT... HE'S TAKEN TO HIS BED...
SO HAVE I...WHEN I THINK OF HOW I HURT HIS FEELINGS, I WANT TO DIE..I FEEL AWFUL... I REALLY OFFENDED HIM...
IN FIRST-AID CLASS I LEARNED THAT IF YOU HAVE OFFENDED SOMEONE, THE BEST TREATMENT IS TO APOLOGIZE IMMEDIATELY..
SCHULZ

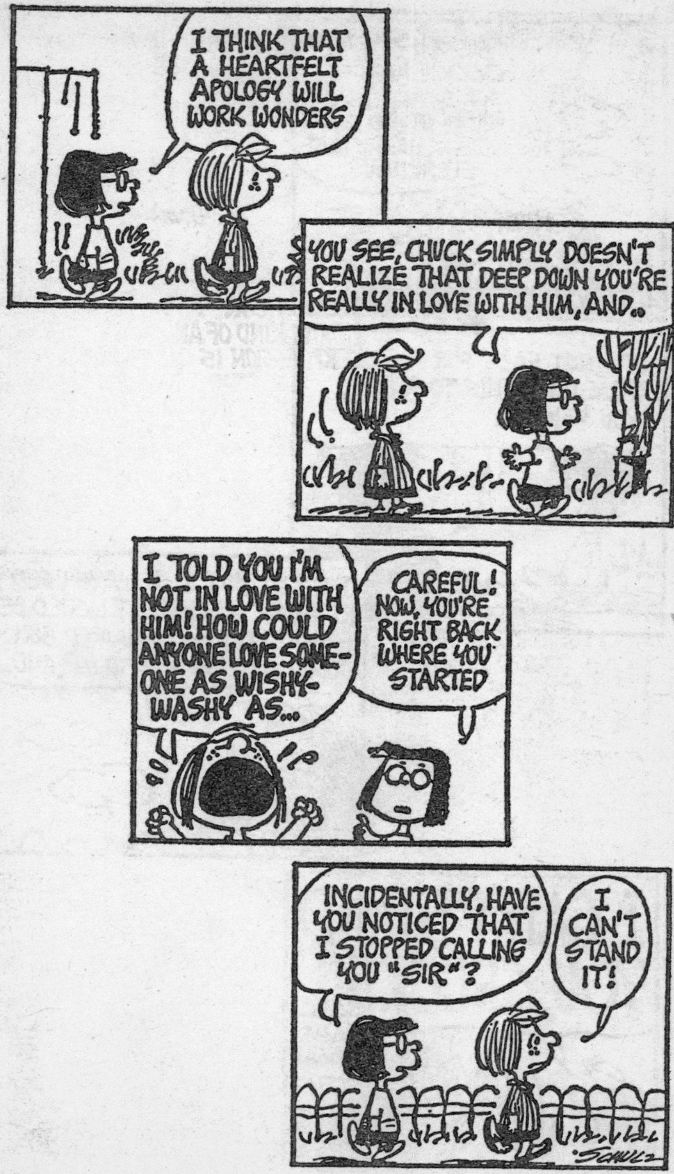
I THINK THAT A HEARTFELT APOLOGY WILL WORK WONDERS
YOU SEE, CHUCK SIMPLY DOESN'T REALIZE THAT DEEP DOWN YOU'RE REALLY IN LOVE WITH HIM, AND..
I TOLD YOU I'M NOT IN LOVE WITH HIM! HOW COULD ANYONE LOVE SOMEONE AS WISHY-WASHY AS...
CAREFUL! NOW, YOU'RE RIGHT BACK WHERE YOU STARTED
INCIDENTALLY, HAVE YOU NOTICED THAT I STOPPED CALLING YOU "SIR"?
I CAN'T STAND IT!
SCHULZ

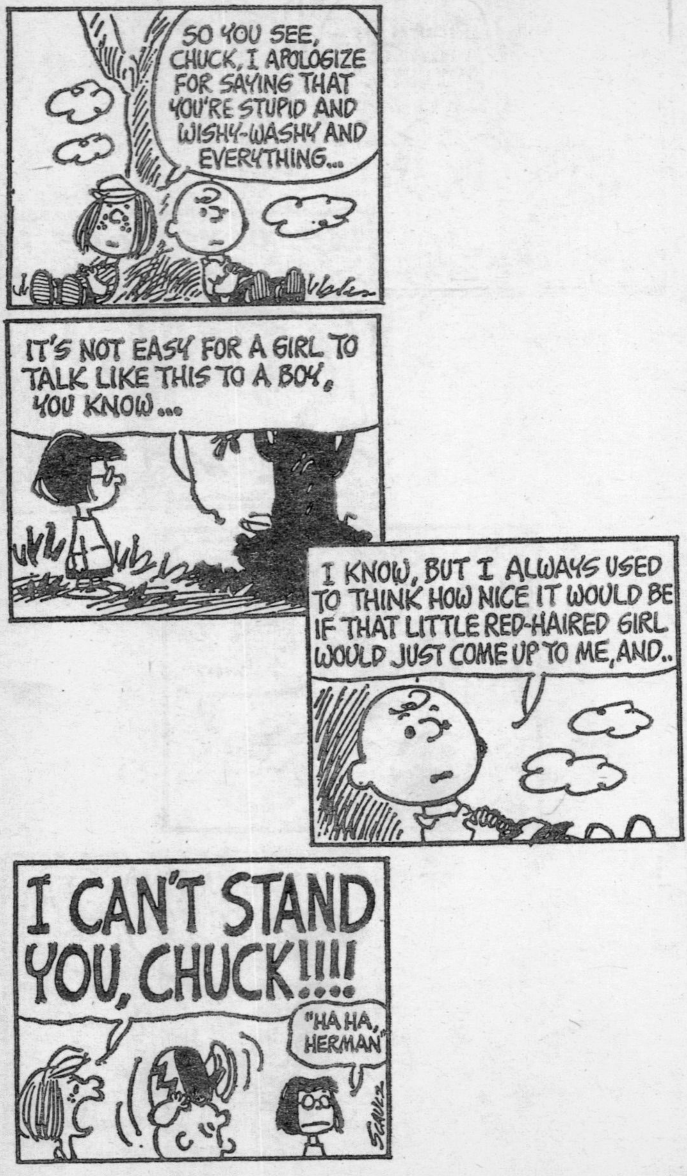
SO YOU SEE, CHUCK, I APOLOGIZE FOR SAYING THAT YOU'RE STUPID AND WISHY-WASHY AND EVERYTHING...
IT'S NOT EASY FOR A GIRL TO TALK LIKE THIS TO A BOY, YOU KNOW...
I KNOW, BUT I ALWAYS USED TO THINK HOW NICE IT WOULD BE IF THAT LITTLE RED-HAIRED GIRL WOULD JUST COME UP TO ME, AND..
I CAN'T STAND YOU, CHUCK!!!!
"HA HA, HERMAN"

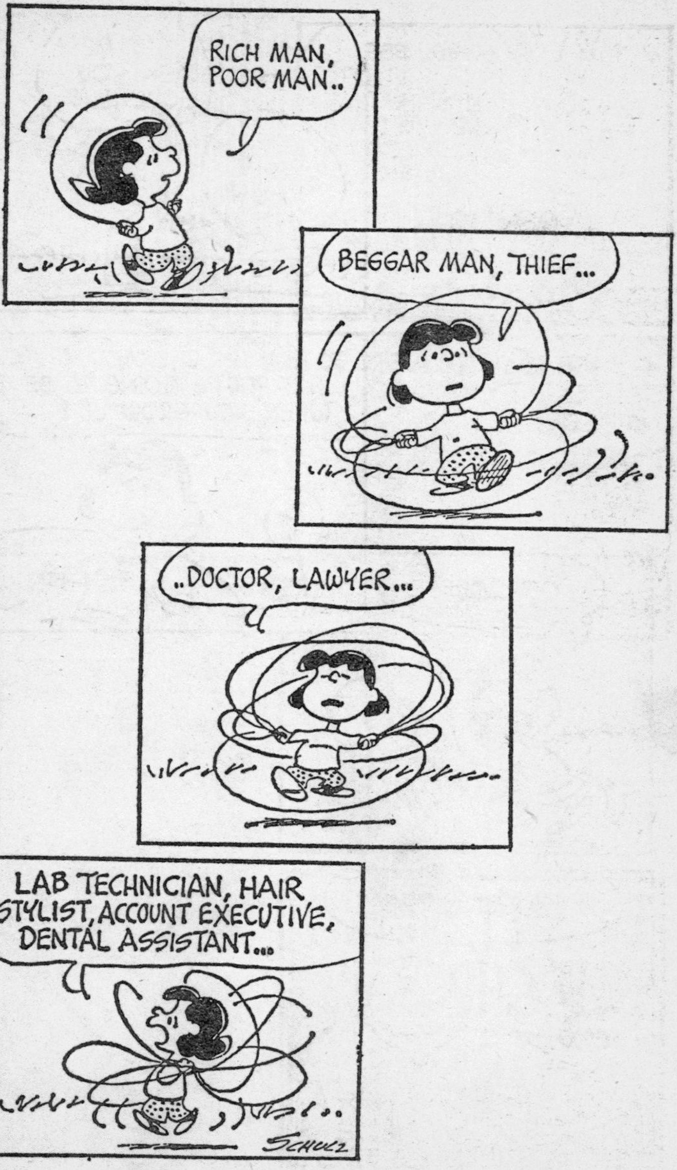
RICH MAN, POOR MAN..
BEGGAR MAN, THIEF...
..DOCTOR, LAWYER...
LAB TECHNICIAN, HAIR STYLIST, ACCOUNT EXECUTIVE, DENTAL ASSISTANT...
SCHULZ

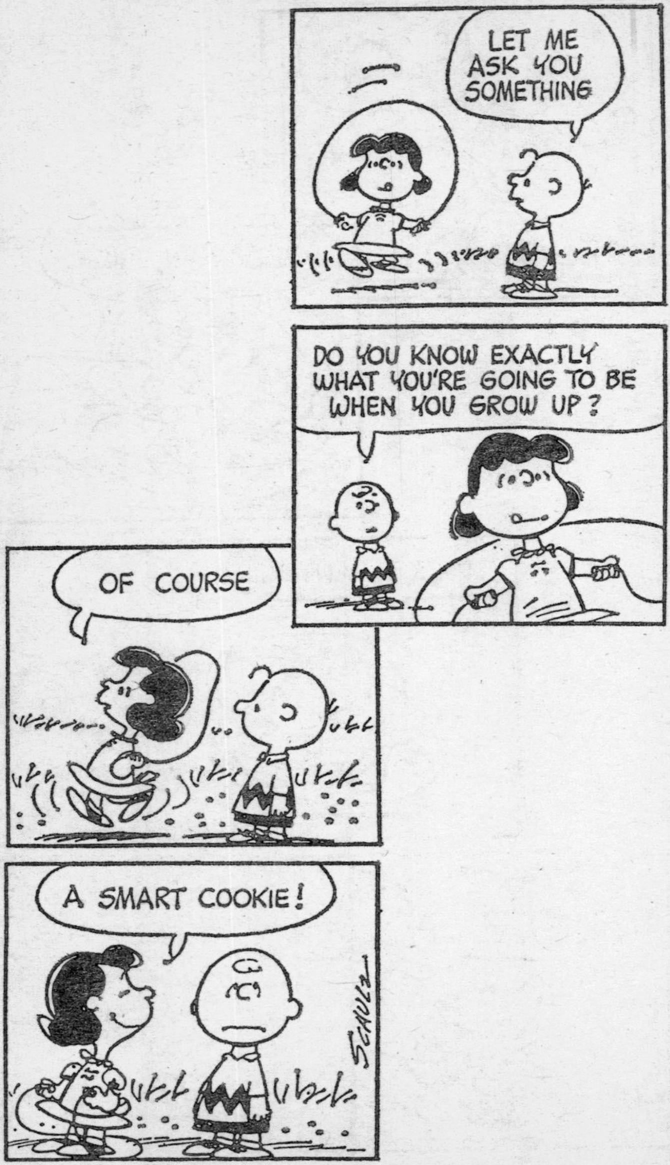
LET ME ASK YOU SOMETHING
DO YOU KNOW EXACTLY WHAT YOU'RE GOING TO BE WHEN YOU GROW UP?
OF COURSE
A SMART COOKIE!
SCHULZ

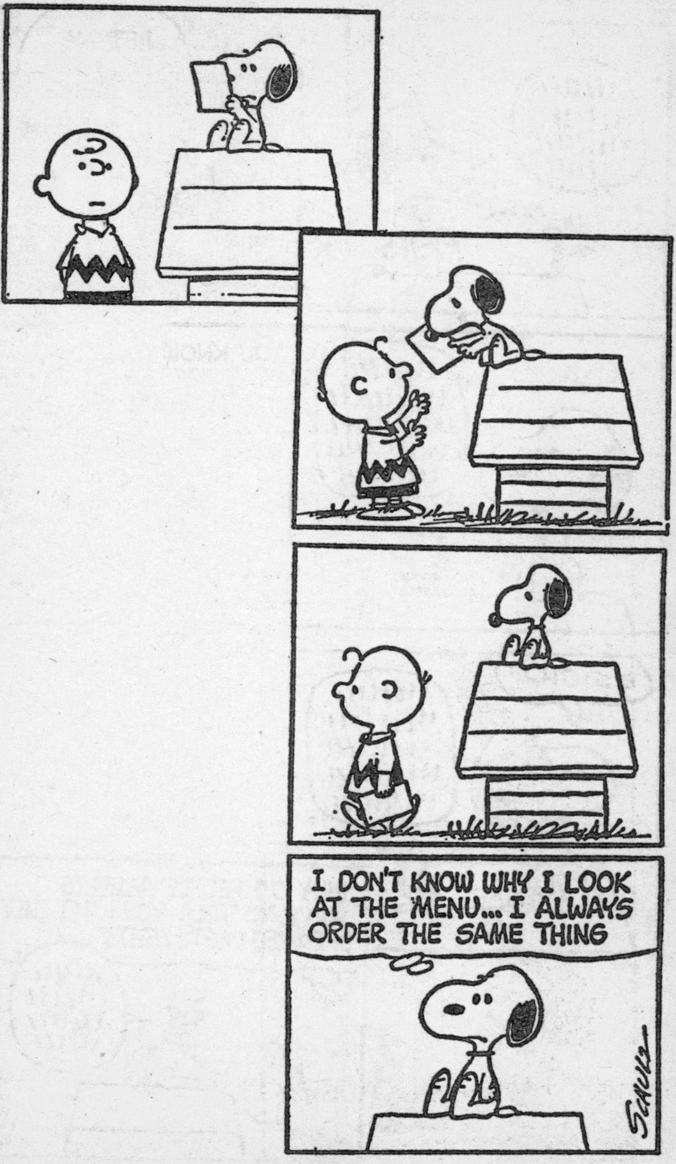
I DON'T KNOW WHY I LOOK AT THE MENU... I ALWAYS ORDER THE SAME THING
SCHULZ

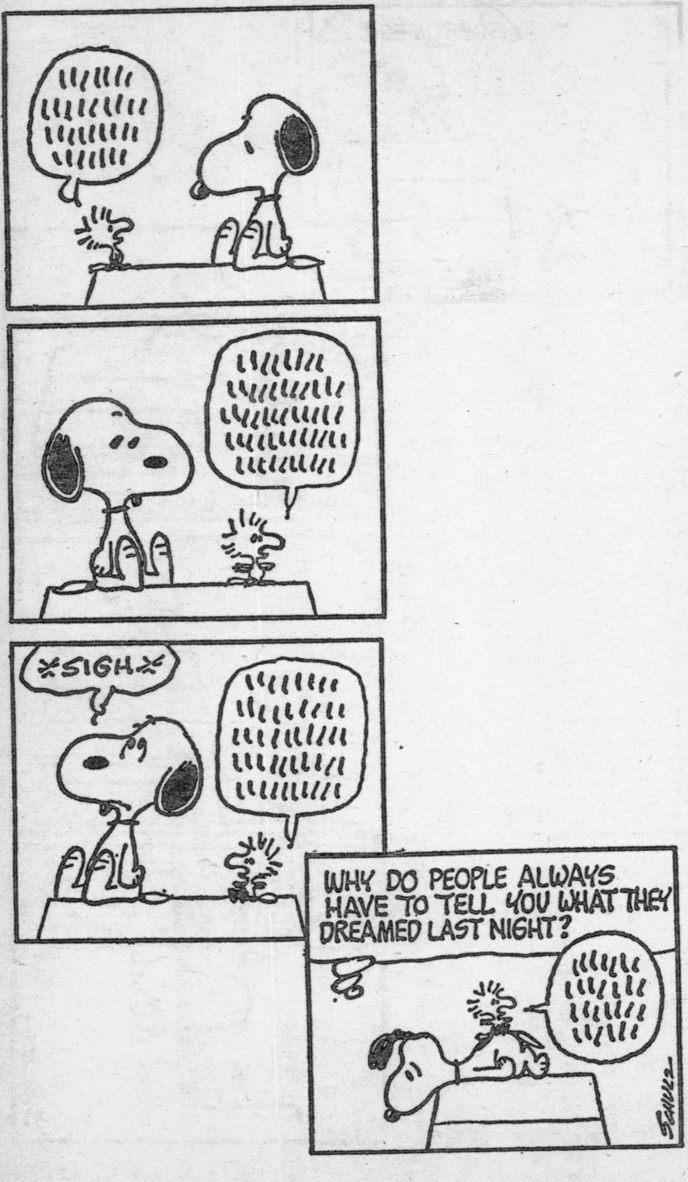
SIGH
WHY DO PEOPLE ALWAYS HAVE TO TELL YOU WHAT THEY DREAMED LAST NIGHT?
SCHULZ

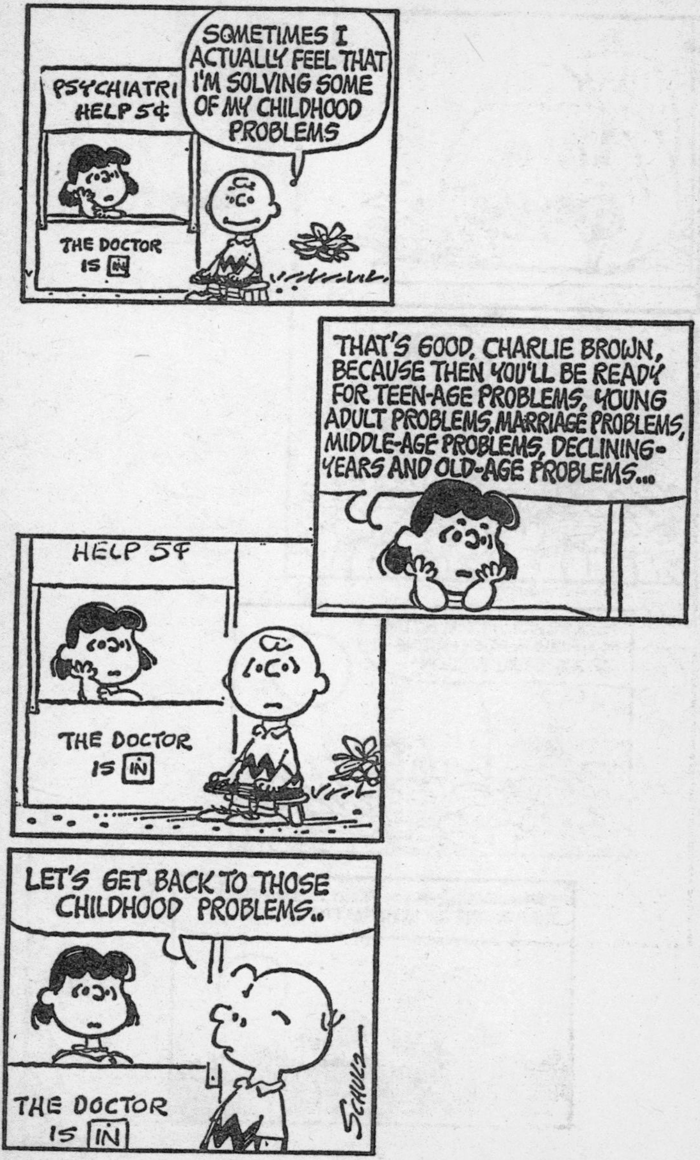
PSYCHIATRI HELP 5¢
SOMETIMES I ACTUALLY FEEL THAT I'M SOLVING SOME OF MY CHILDHOOD PROBLEMS
THE DOCTOR IS IN
THAT'S GOOD, CHARLIE BROWN, BECAUSE THEN YOU'LL BE READY FOR TEEN-AGE PROBLEMS, YOUNG ADULT PROBLEMS, MARRIAGE PROBLEMS, MIDDLE-AGE PROBLEMS, DECLINING-YEARS AND OLD-AGE PROBLEMS...
HELP 5¢
THE DOCTOR IS IN
LET'S GET BACK TO THOSE CHILDHOOD PROBLEMS..
THE DOCTOR IS IN
SCHULZ

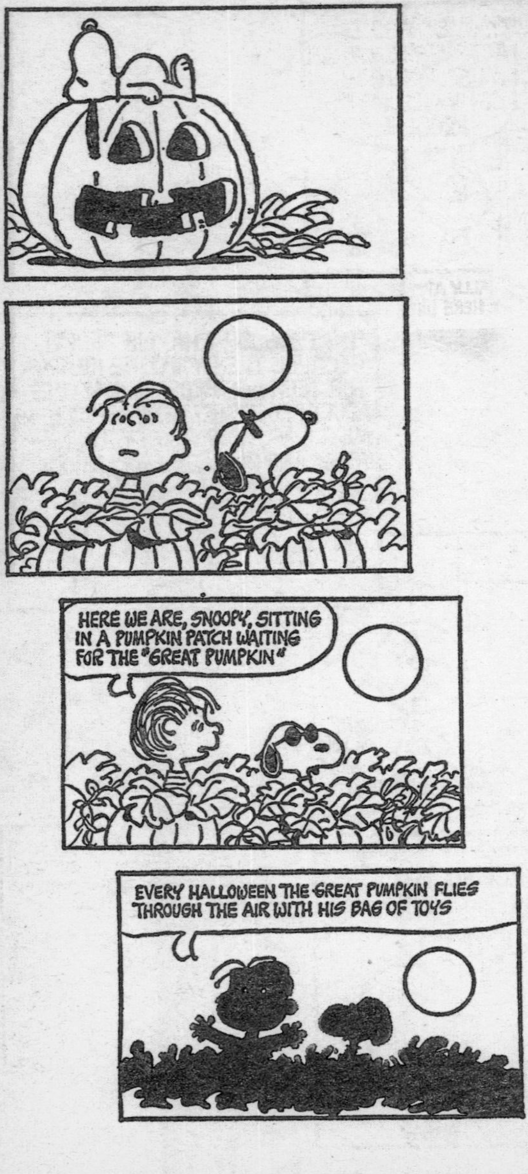
HERE WE ARE, SNOOPY, SITTING IN A PUMPKIN PATCH WAITING FOR THE "GREAT PUMPKIN"
EVERY HALLOWEEN THE GREAT PUMPKIN FLIES THROUGH THE AIR WITH HIS BAG OF TOYS

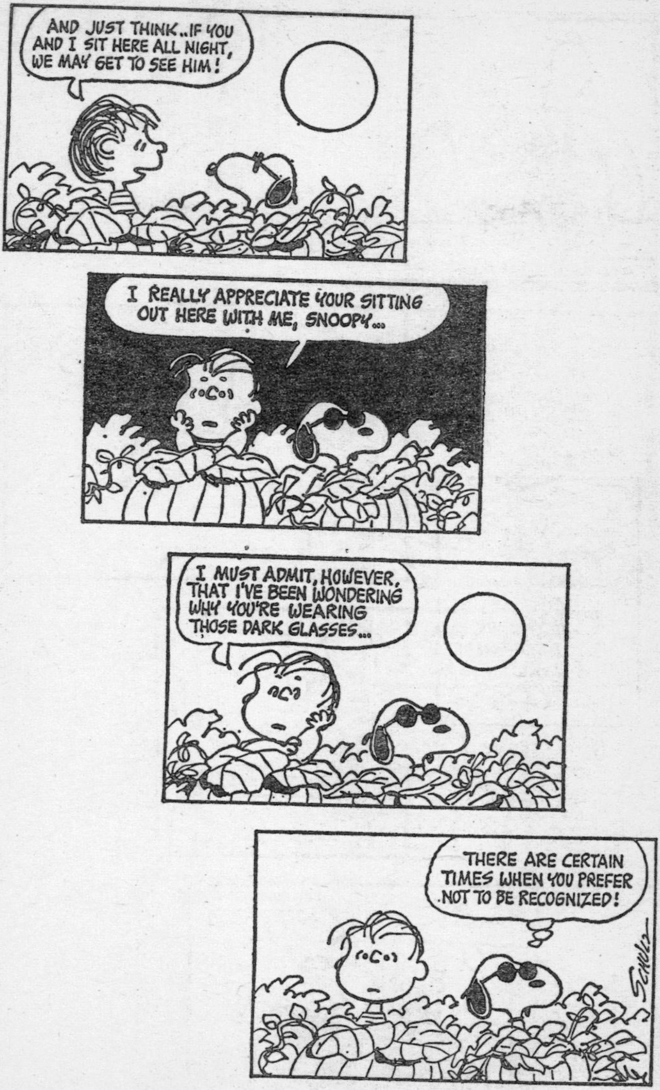
AND JUST THINK..IF YOU AND I SIT HERE ALL NIGHT, WE MAY GET TO SEE HIM!
I REALLY APPRECIATE YOUR SITTING OUT HERE WITH ME, SNOOPY...
I MUST ADMIT, HOWEVER, THAT I'VE BEEN WONDERING WHY YOU'RE WEARING THOSE DARK GLASSES...
THERE ARE CERTAIN TIMES WHEN YOU PREFER NOT TO BE RECOGNIZED!
SCHULZ

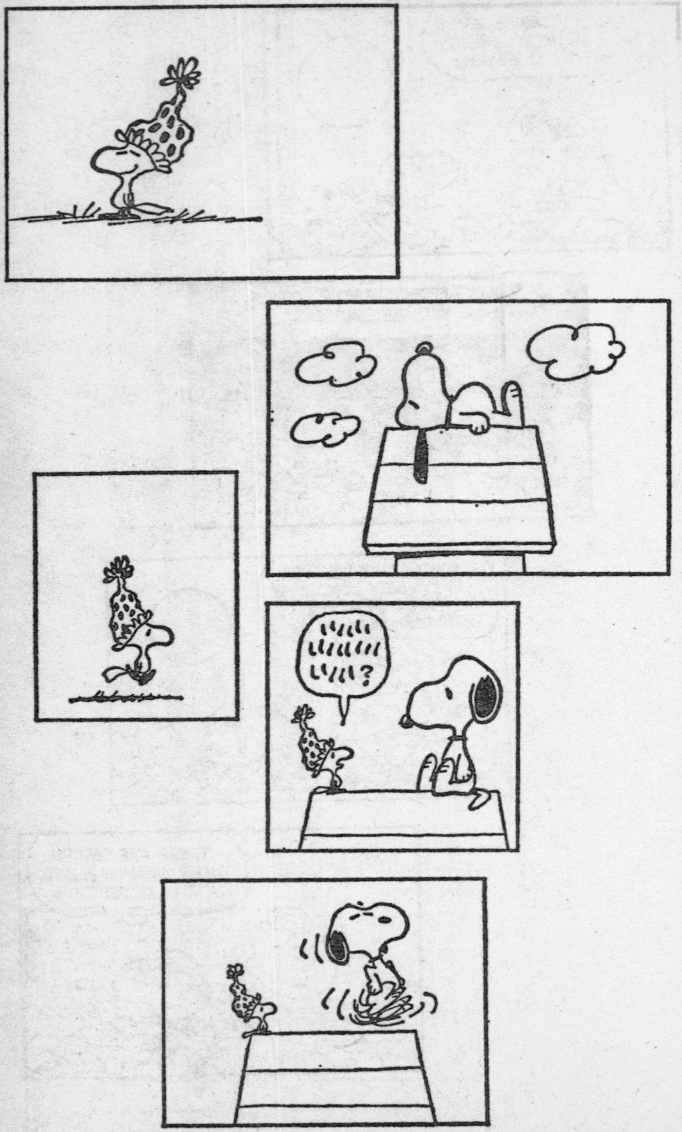

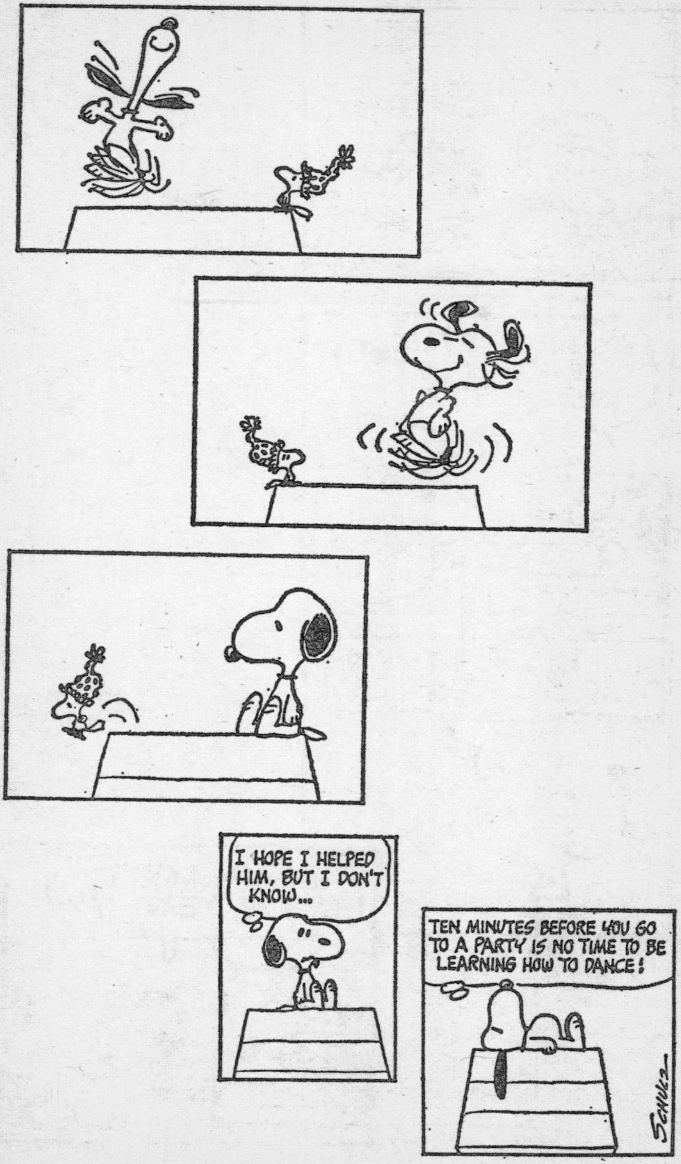
I HOPE I HELPED HIM, BUT I DON'T KNOW...
TEN MINUTES BEFORE YOU GO TO A PARTY IS NO TIME TO BE LEARNING HOW TO DANCE!
SCHULZ

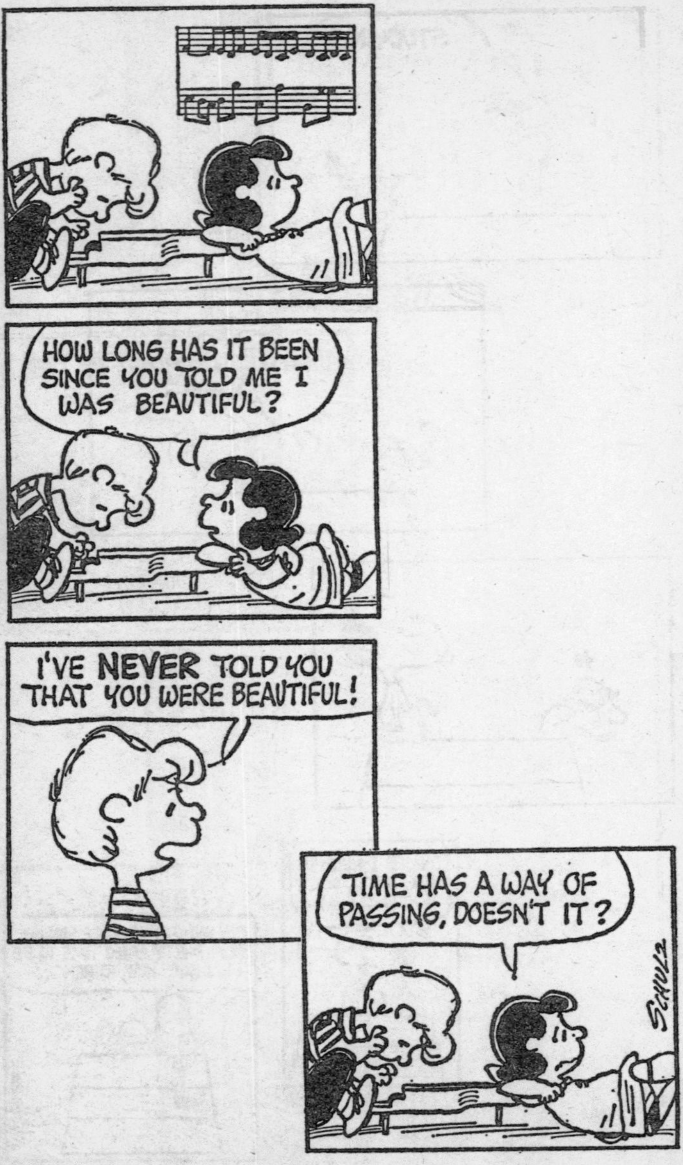
HOW LONG HAS IT BEEN SINCE YOU TOLD ME I WAS BEAUTIFUL?
I'VE NEVER TOLD YOU THAT YOU WERE BEAUTIFUL!
TIME HAS A WAY OF PASSING, DOESN'T IT?
SCHULZ

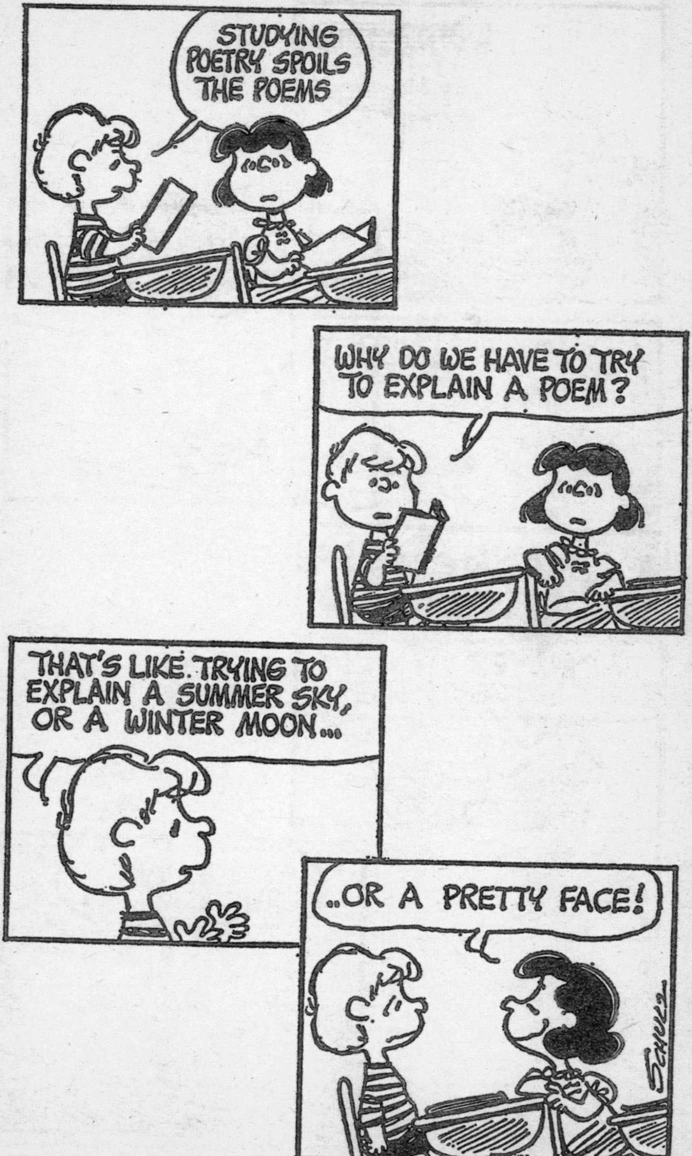
STUDYING POETRY SPOILS THE POEMS
WHY DO WE HAVE TO TRY TO EXPLAIN A POEM?
THAT'S LIKE TRYING TO EXPLAIN A SUMMER SKY, OR A WINTER MOON...
..OR A PRETTY FACE!
SCHULZ

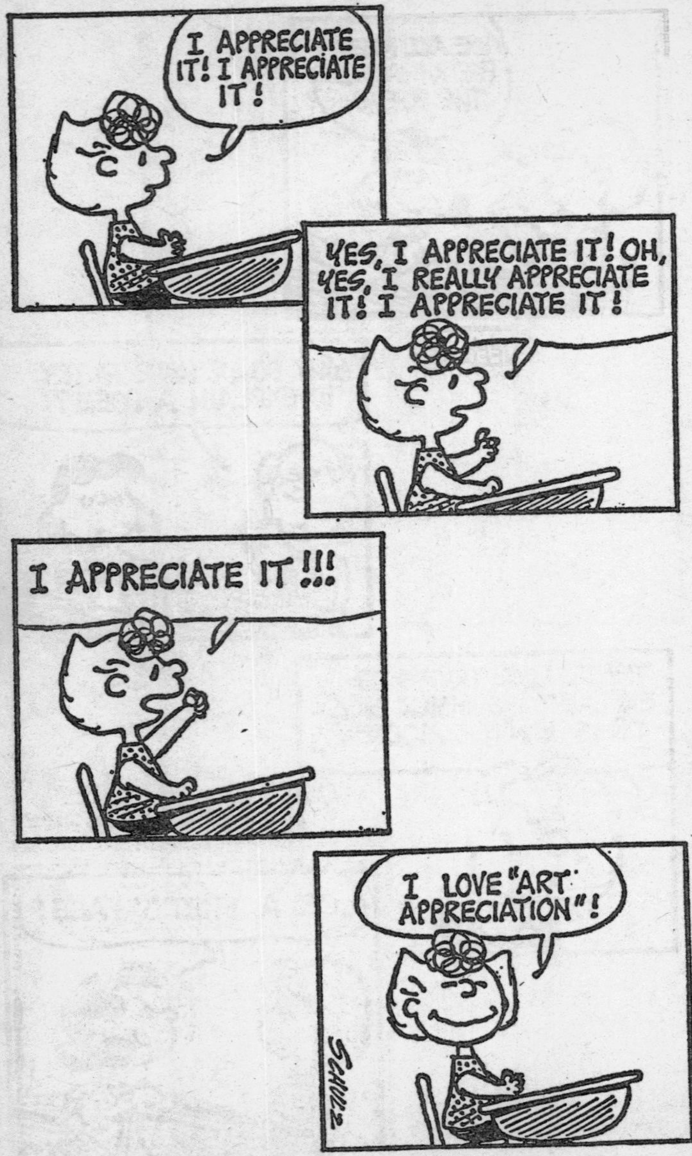
I APPRECIATE IT! I APPRECIATE IT!
YES, I APPRECIATE IT! OH, YES, I REALLY APPRECIATE IT! I APPRECIATE IT!
I APPRECIATE IT!!!
I LOVE "ART APPRECIATION"!
SCHULZ

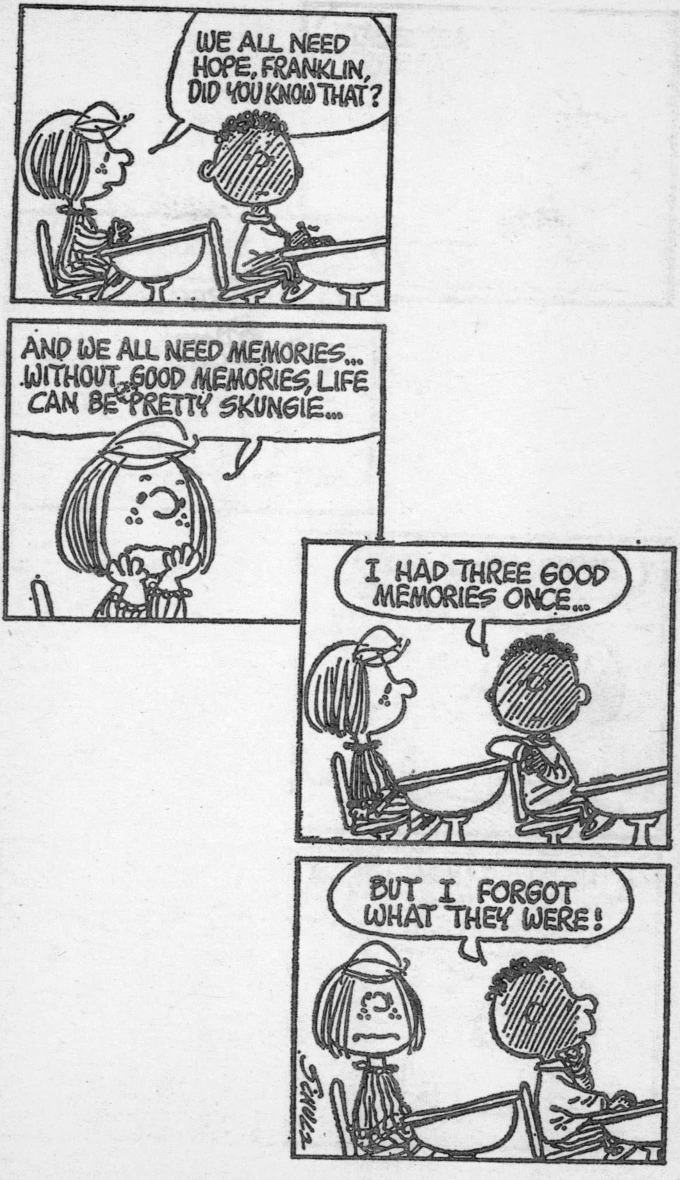
WE ALL NEED HOPE, FRANKLIN, DID YOU KNOW THAT?
AND WE ALL NEED MEMORIES... WITHOUT GOOD MEMORIES, LIFE CAN BE PRETTY SKUNGIE...
I HAD THREE GOOD MEMORIES ONCE...
BUT I FORGOT WHAT THEY WERE!

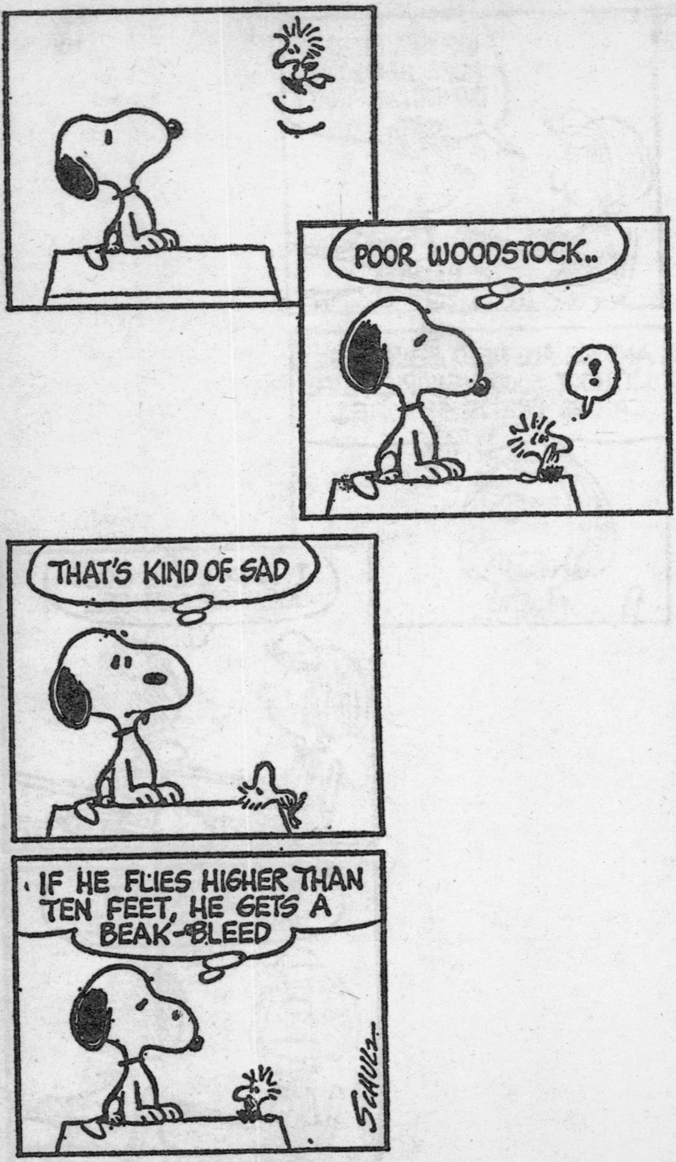
POOR WOODSTOCK..
!
THAT'S KIND OF SAD
IF HE FLIES HIGHER THAN TEN FEET, HE GETS A BEAK-BLEED
SCHULZ

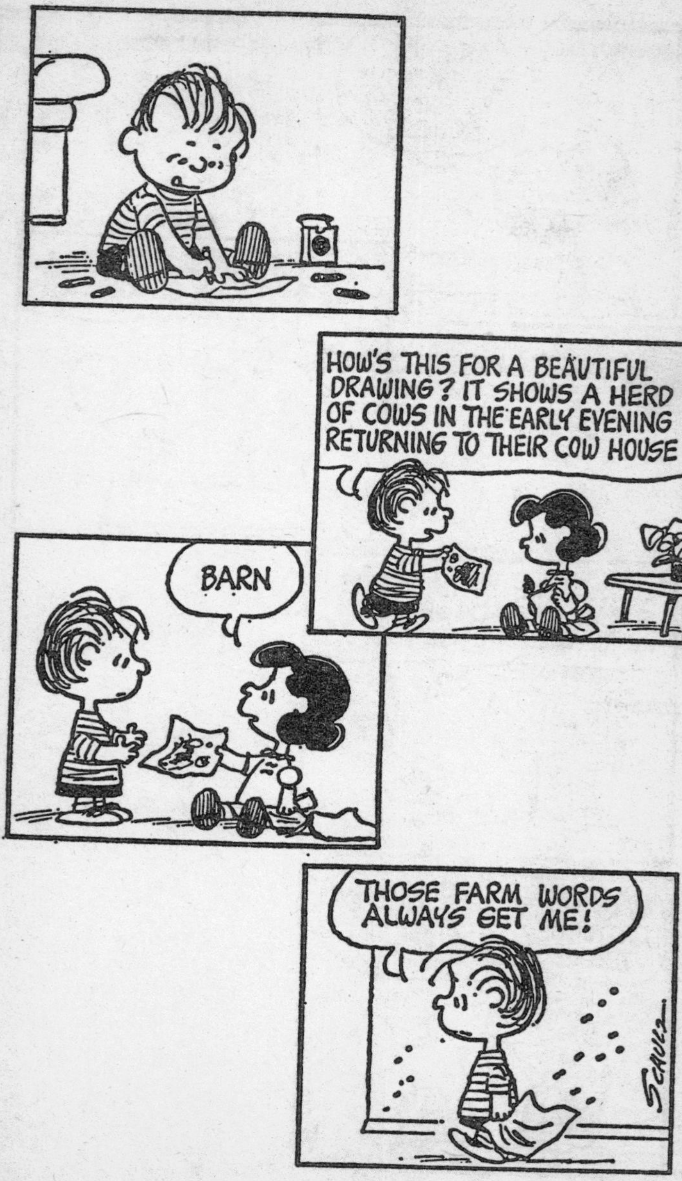
HOW'S THIS FOR A BEAUTIFUL DRAWING? IT SHOWS A HERD OF COWS IN THE EARLY EVENING RETURNING TO THEIR COW HOUSE
BARN
THOSE FARM WORDS ALWAYS GET ME!
SCHULZ

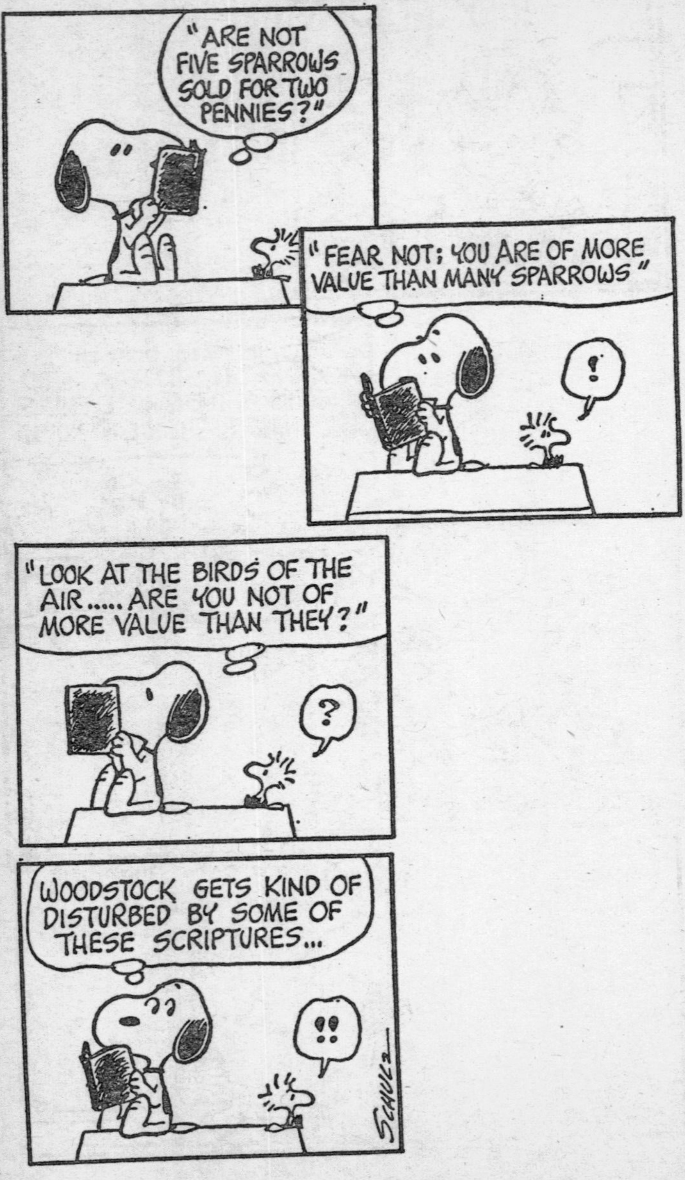
"ARE NOT FIVE SPARROWS SOLD FOR TWO PENNIES?"
"FEAR NOT; YOU ARE OF MORE VALUE THAN MANY SPARROWS"
!
"LOOK AT THE BIRDS OF THE AIR..... ARE YOU NOT OF MORE VALUE THAN THEY?"
?
WOODSTOCK GETS KIND OF DISTURBED BY SOME OF THESE SCRIPTURES...
!!
SCHULZ

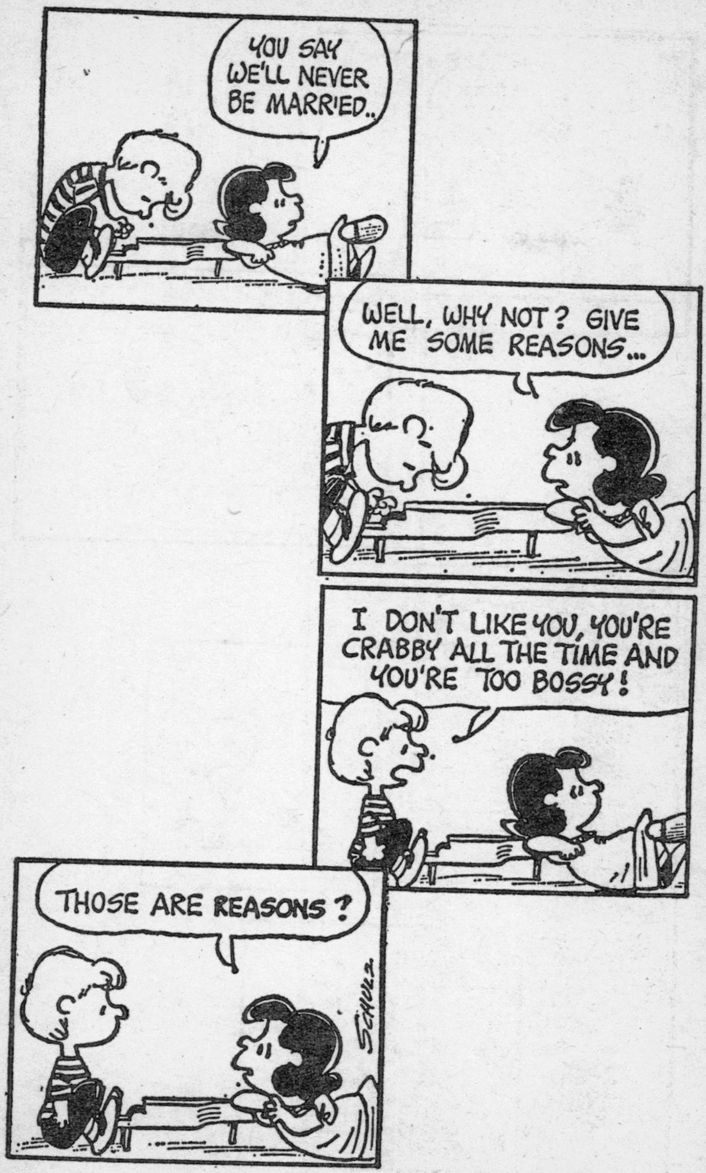
YOU SAY WE'LL NEVER BE MARRIED..
WELL, WHY NOT? GIVE ME SOME REASONS...
I DON'T LIKE YOU, YOU'RE CRABBY ALL THE TIME AND YOU'RE TOO BOSSY!
THOSE ARE REASONS?
SCHULZ

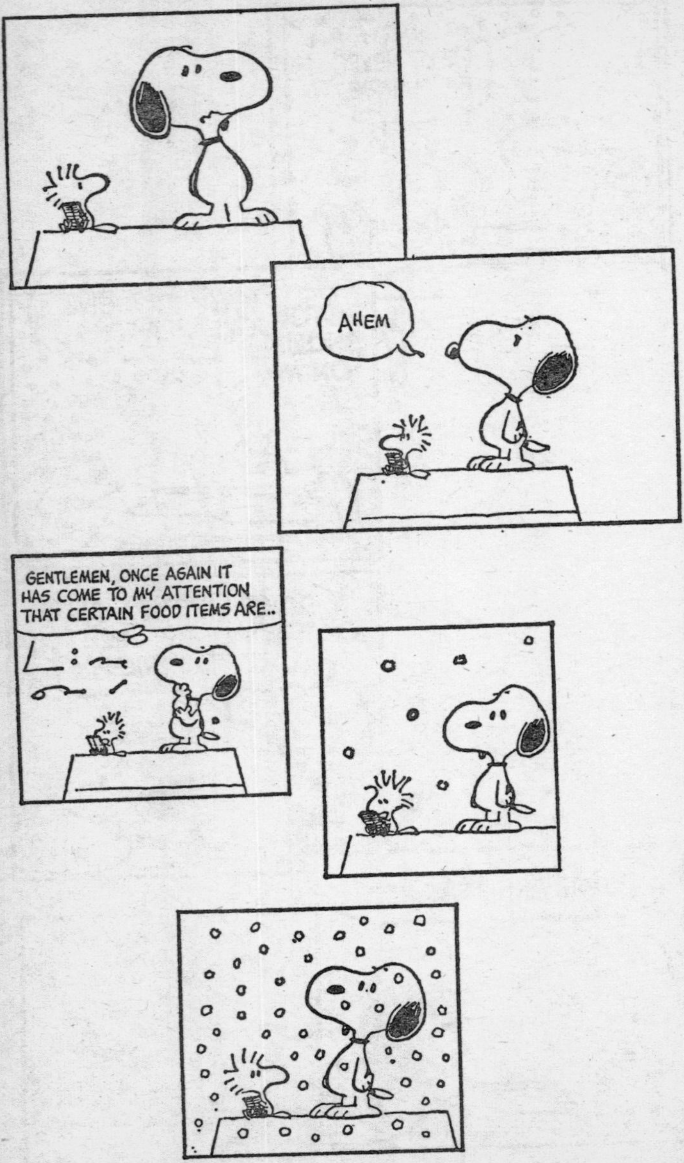
AHEM
GENTLEMEN, ONCE AGAIN IT HAS COME TO MY ATTENTION THAT CERTAIN FOOD ITEMS ARE..

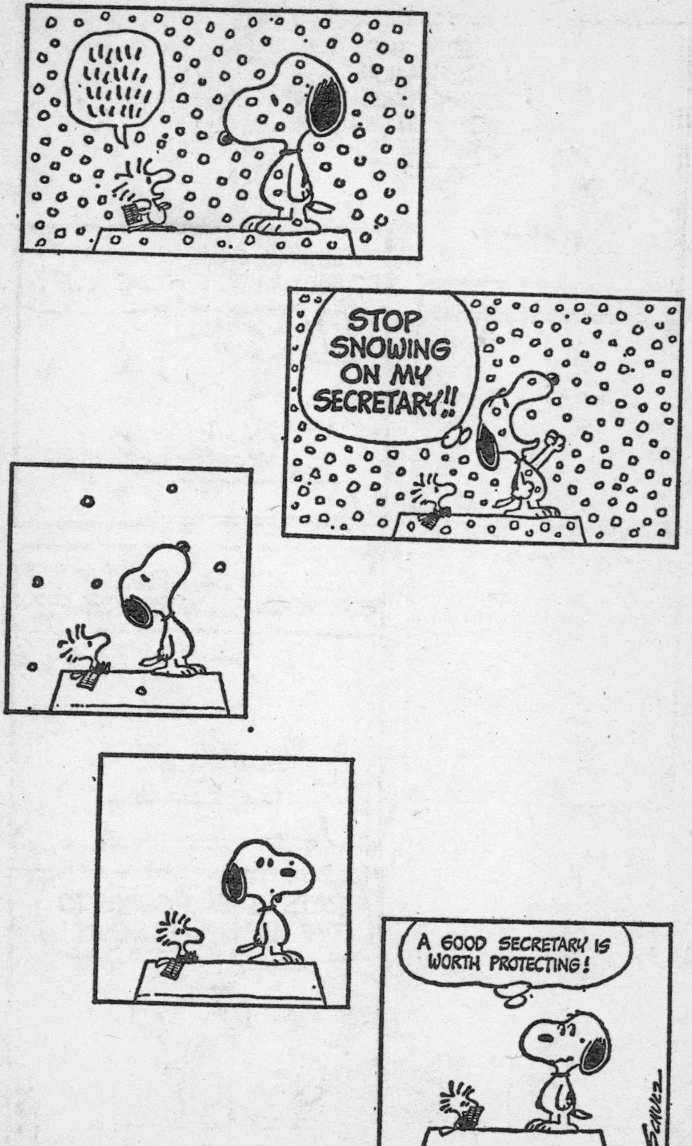
STOP SNOWING ON MY SECRETARY!!
A GOOD SECRETARY IS WORTH PROTECTING!
SCHULZ

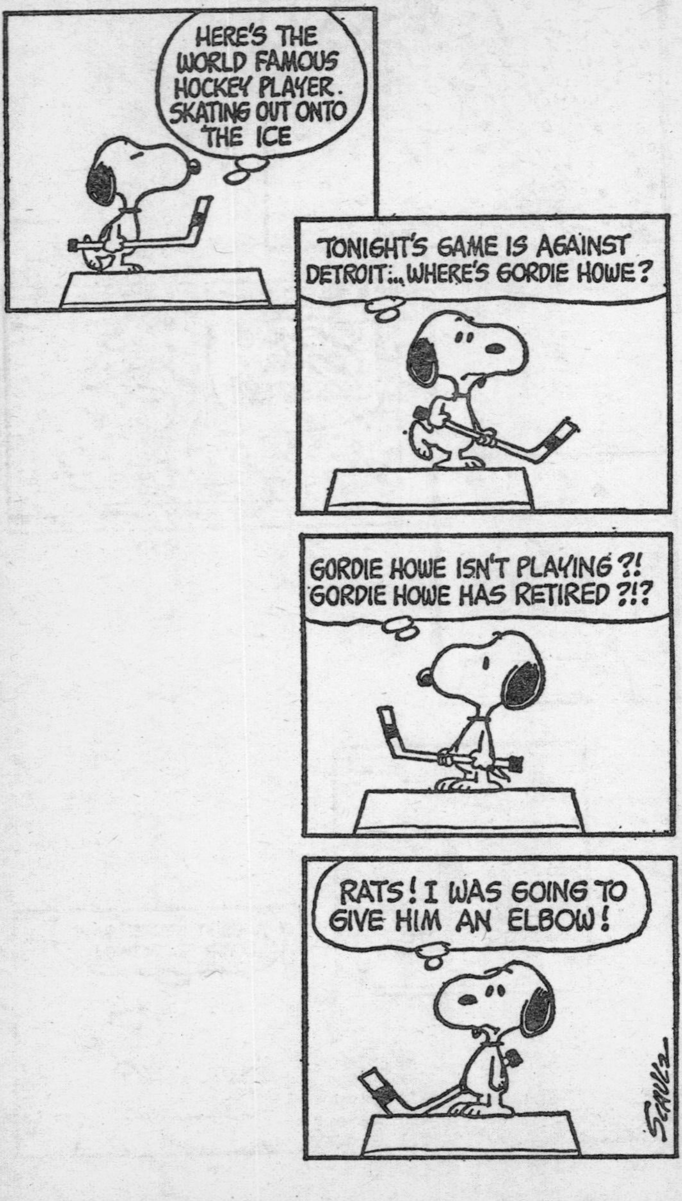
HERE'S THE WORLD FAMOUS HOCKEY PLAYER. SKATING OUT ONTO THE ICE
TONIGHT'S GAME IS AGAINST DETROIT:.. WHERE'S GORDIE HOWE?
GORDIE HOWE ISN'T PLAYING?! GORDIE HOWE HAS RETIRED?!?
RATS! I WAS GOING TO GIVE HIM AN ELBOW!
SCHULZ

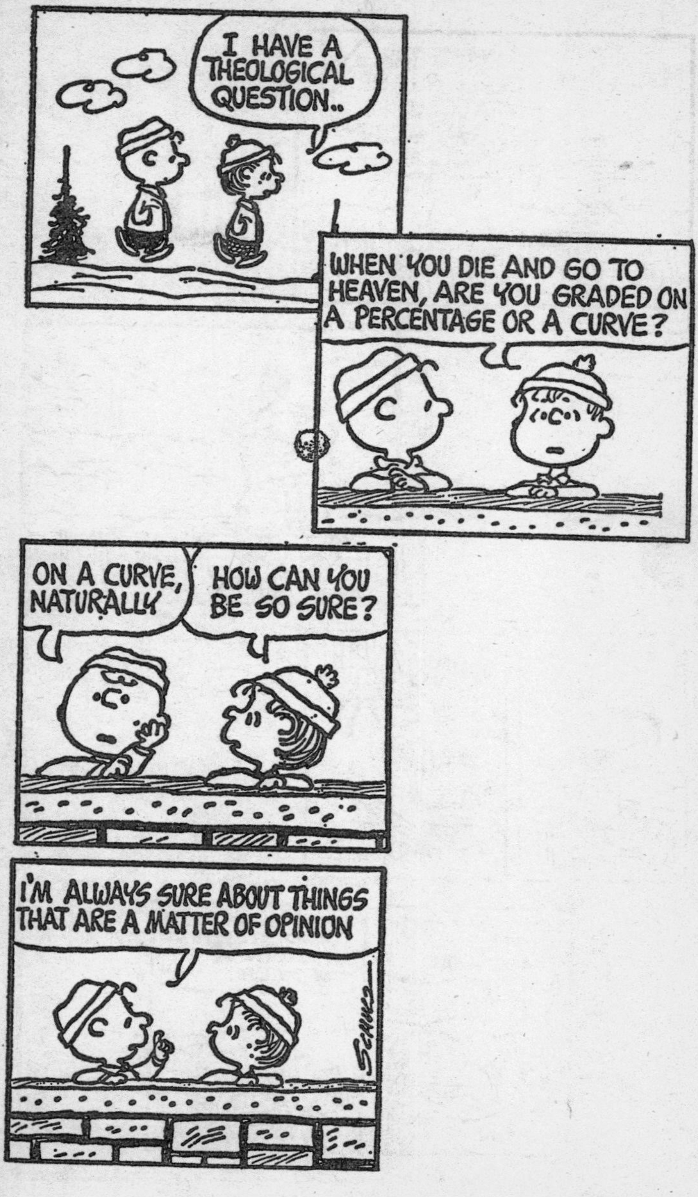
I HAVE A THEOLOGICAL QUESTION..
WHEN YOU DIE AND GO TO HEAVEN, ARE YOU GRADED ON A PERCENTAGE OR A CURVE?
ON A CURVE, NATURALLY
HOW CAN YOU BE SO SURE?
I'M ALWAYS SURE ABOUT THINGS THAT ARE A MATTER OF OPINION
SCHULZ

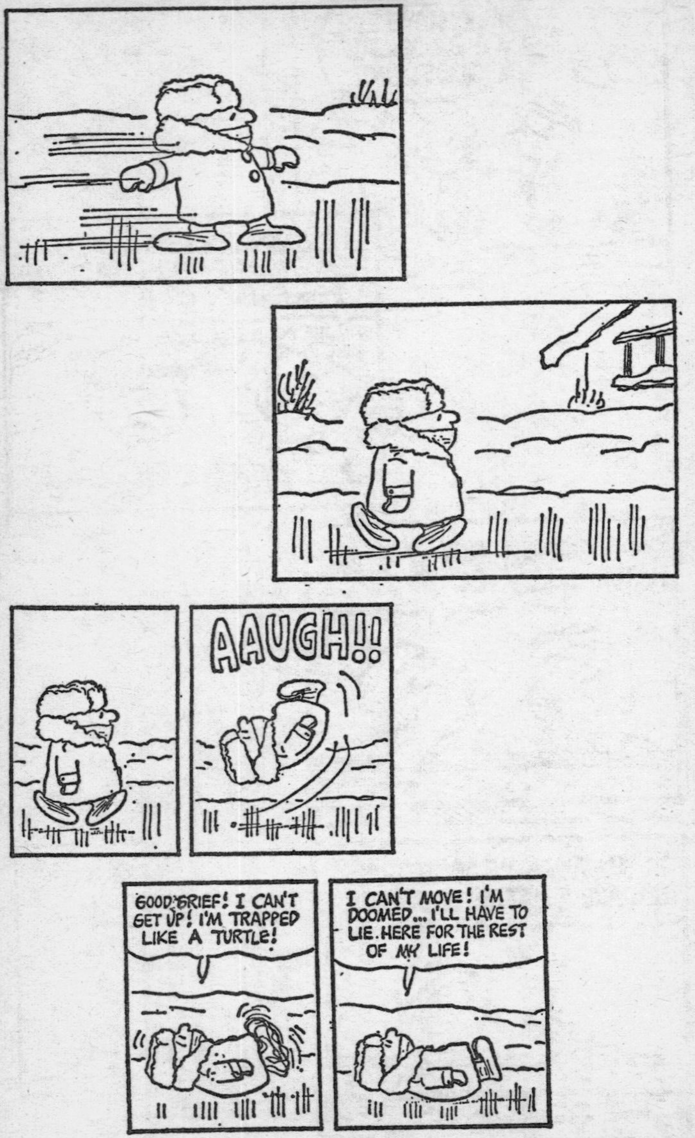
AAUGH!!
GOOD GRIEF! I CAN'T GET UP! I'M TRAPPED LIKE A TURTLE!
I CAN'T MOVE! I'M DOOMED... I'LL HAVE TO LIE HERE FOR THE REST OF MY LIFE!

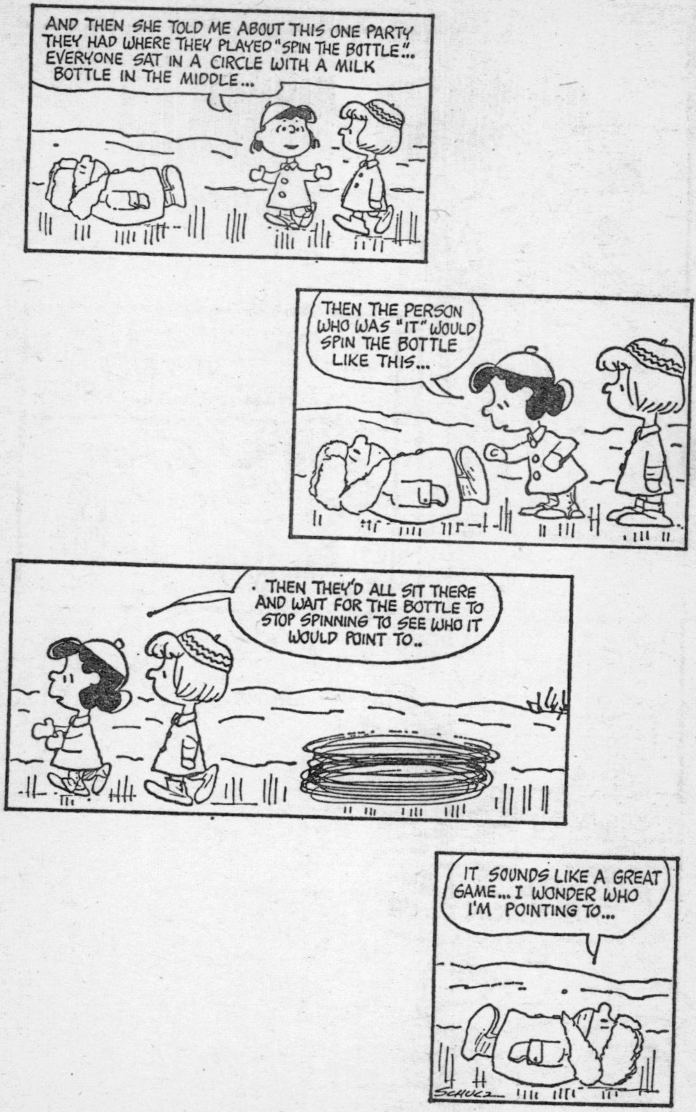
AND THEN SHE TOLD ME ABOUT THIS ONE PARTY THEY HAD WHERE THEY PLAYED "SPIN THE BOTTLE"... EVERYONE SAT IN A CIRCLE WITH A MILK BOTTLE IN THE MIDDLE...
THEN THE PERSON WHO WAS "IT" WOULD SPIN THE BOTTLE LIKE THIS...
THEN THEY'D ALL SIT THERE AND WAIT FOR THE BOTTLE TO STOP SPINNING TO SEE WHO IT WOULD POINT TO..
IT SOUNDS LIKE A GREAT GAME... I WONDER WHO I'M POINTING TO...
SCHULZ

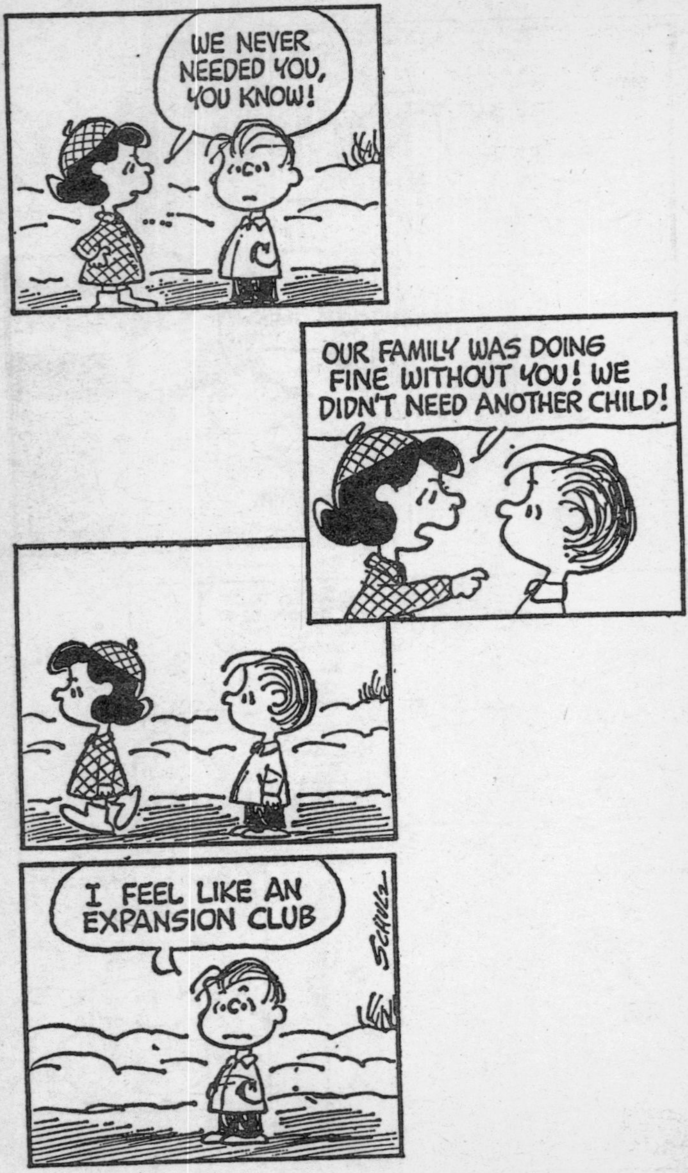
WE NEVER NEEDED YOU, YOU KNOW!
OUR FAMILY WAS DOING FINE WITHOUT YOU! WE DIDN'T NEED ANOTHER CHILD!
I FEEL LIKE AN EXPANSION CLUB
SCHULZ

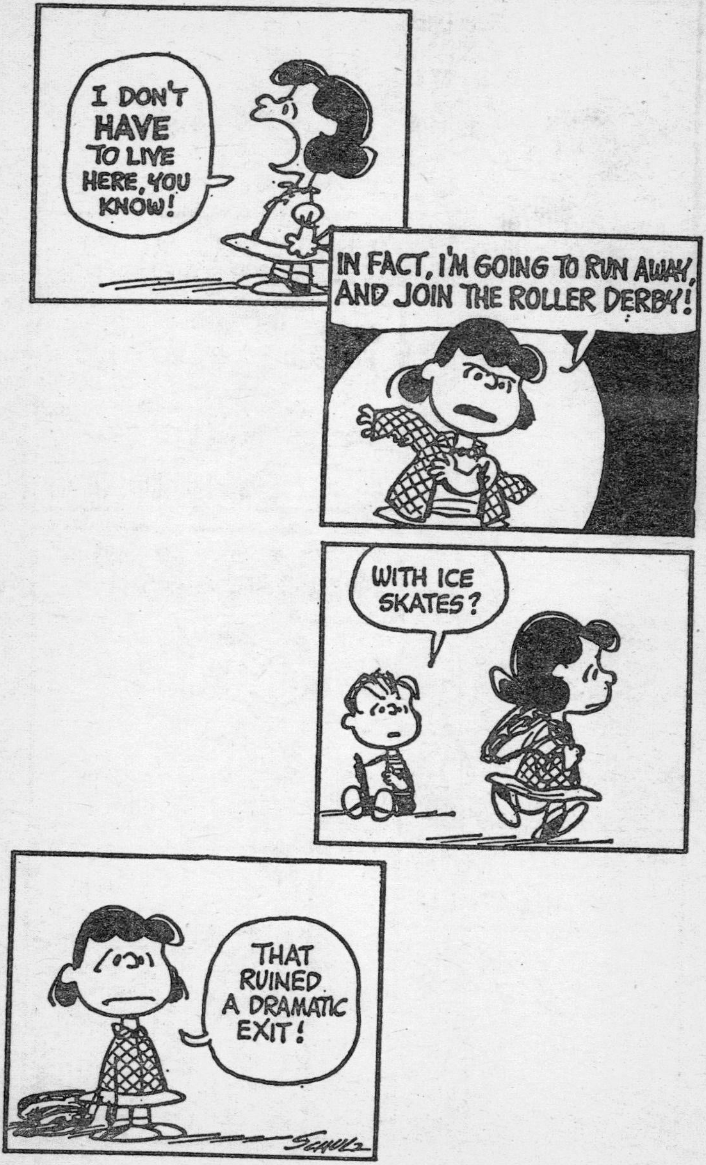
I DON'T HAVE TO LIVE HERE, YOU KNOW!
IN FACT, I'M GOING TO RUN AWAY, AND JOIN THE ROLLER DERBY!
WITH ICE SKATES?
THAT RUINED A DRAMATIC EXIT!
SCHULZ

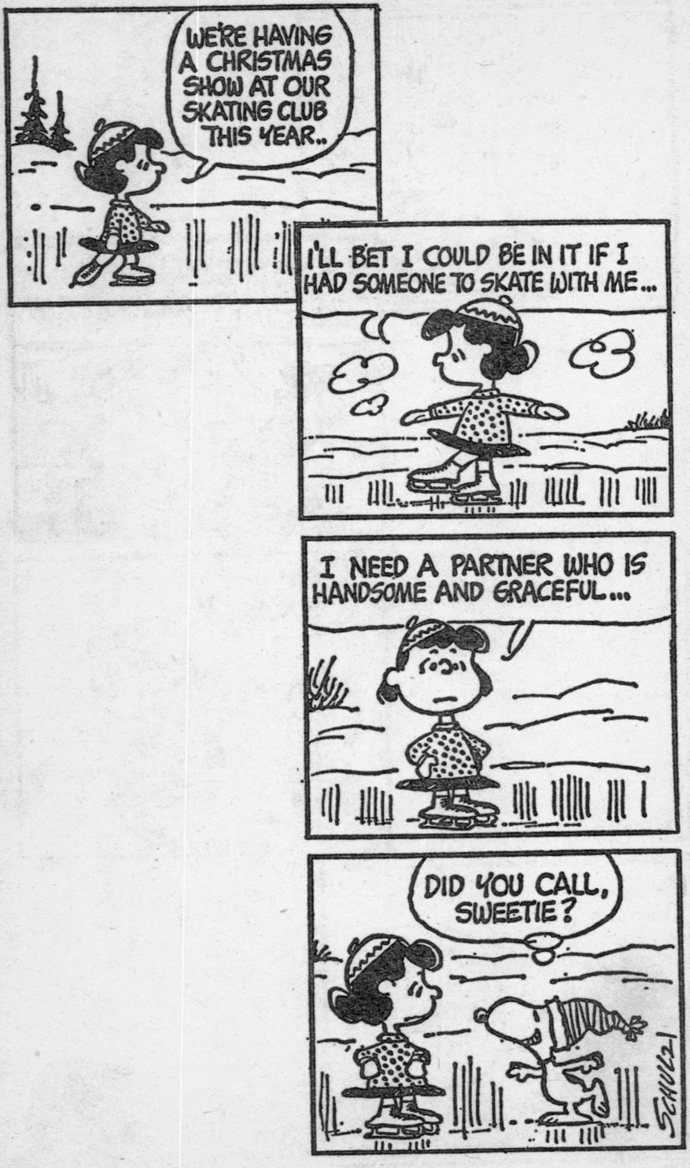
WE'RE HAVING A CHRISTMAS SHOW AT OUR SKATING CLUB THIS YEAR..
I'LL BET I COULD BE IN IT IF I HAD SOMEONE TO SKATE WITH ME...
I NEED A PARTNER WHO IS HANDSOME AND GRACEFUL...
DID YOU CALL, SWEETIE?
SCHULZ

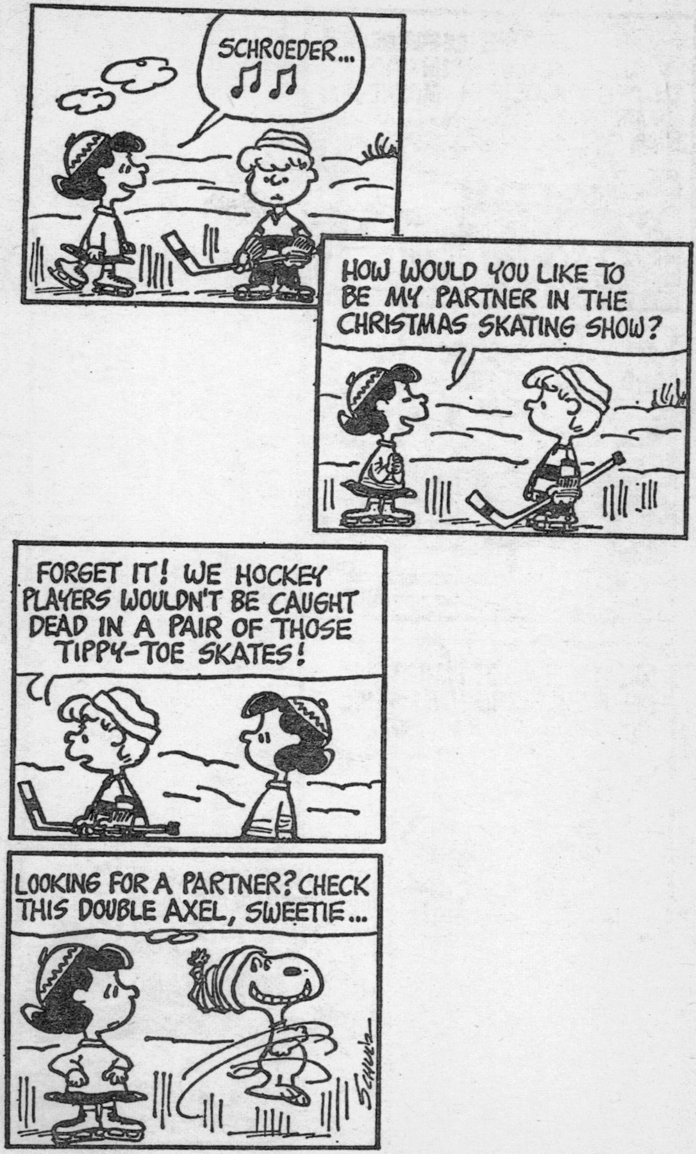
SCHROEDER...
HOW WOULD YOU LIKE TO BE MY PARTNER IN THE CHRISTMAS SKATING SHOW?
FORGET IT! WE HOCKEY PLAYERS WOULDN'T BE CAUGHT DEAD IN A PAIR OF THOSE TIPPY-TOE SKATES!
LOOKING FOR A PARTNER? CHECK THIS DOUBLE AXEL, SWEETIE...
SCHULZ

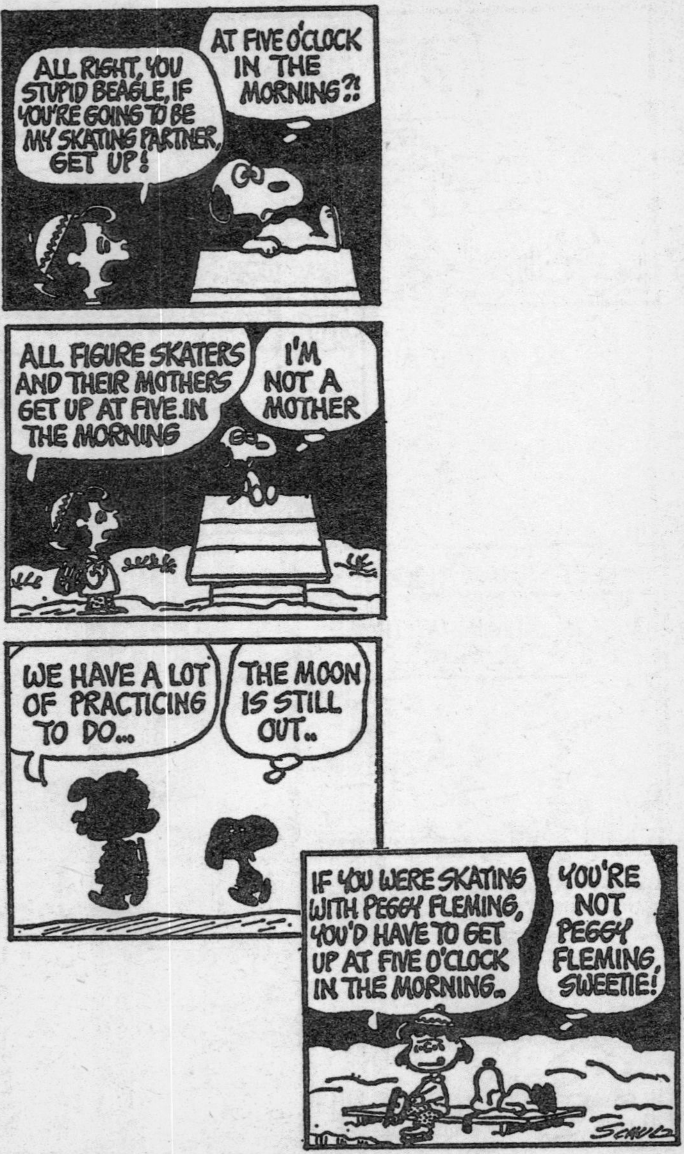
ALL RIGHT, YOU STUPID BEAGLE, IF YOU'RE GOING TO BE MY SKATING PARTNER, GET UP!
AT FIVE O'CLOCK IN THE MORNING?!
ALL FIGURE SKATERS AND THEIR MOTHERS GET UP AT FIVE IN THE MORNING
I'M NOT A MOTHER
WE HAVE A LOT OF PRACTICING TO DO...
THE MOON IS STILL OUT..
IF YOU WERE SKATING WITH PEGGY FLEMING, YOU'D HAVE TO GET UP AT FIVE O'CLOCK IN THE MORNING..
YOU'RE NOT PEGGY FLEMING, SWEETIE!
SCHULZ

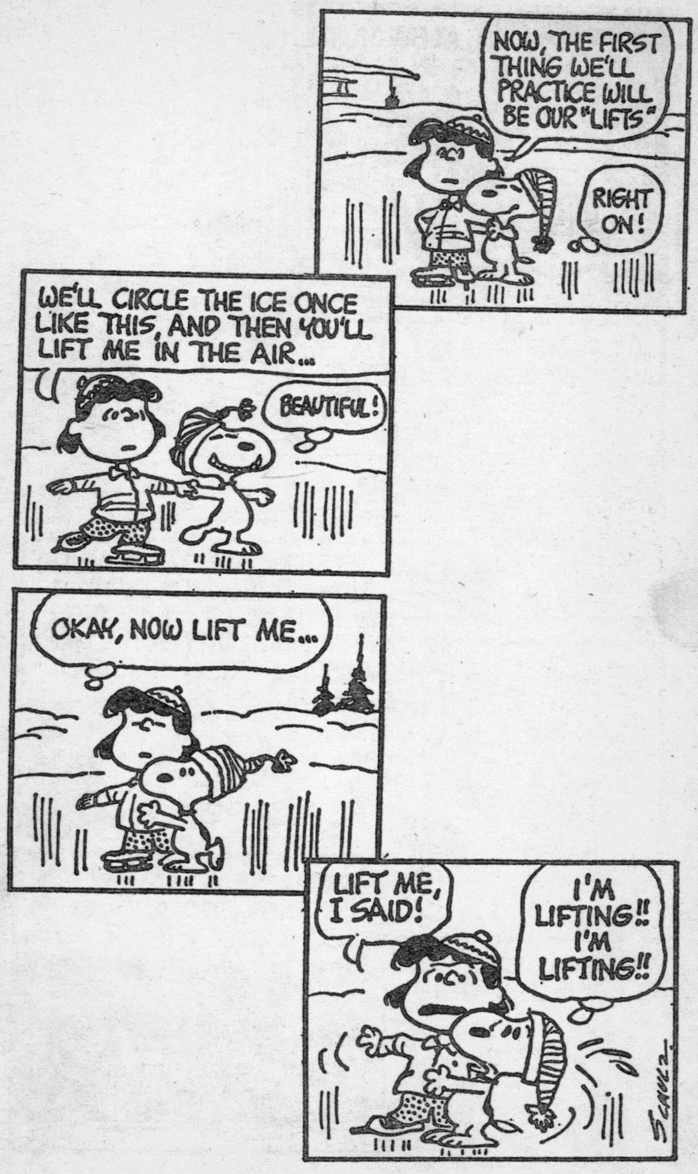
NOW, THE FIRST THING WE'LL PRACTICE WILL BE OUR "LIFTS"
RIGHT ON!
WE'LL CIRCLE THE ICE ONCE LIKE THIS, AND THEN YOU'LL LIFT ME IN THE AIR...
BEAUTIFUL!
OKAY, NOW LIFT ME...
LIFT ME, I SAID!
I'M LIFTING!! I'M LIFTING!!
SCHULZ

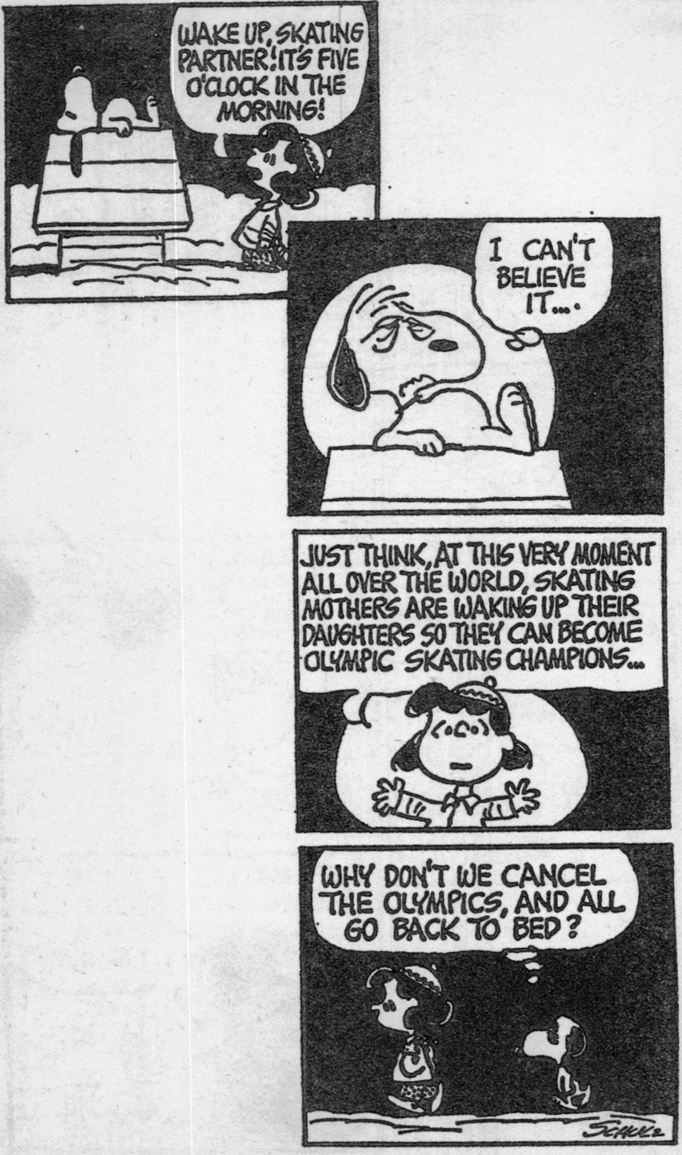
WAKE UP, SKATING PARTNER! IT'S FIVE O'CLOCK IN THE MORNING!
I CAN'T BELIEVE IT....
JUST THINK, AT THIS VERY MOMENT ALL OVER THE WORLD, SKATING MOTHERS ARE WAKING UP THEIR DAUGHTERS SO THEY CAN BECOME OLYMPIC SKATING CHAMPIONS...
WHY DON'T WE CANCEL THE OLYMPICS, AND ALL GO BACK TO BED?
SCHULZ

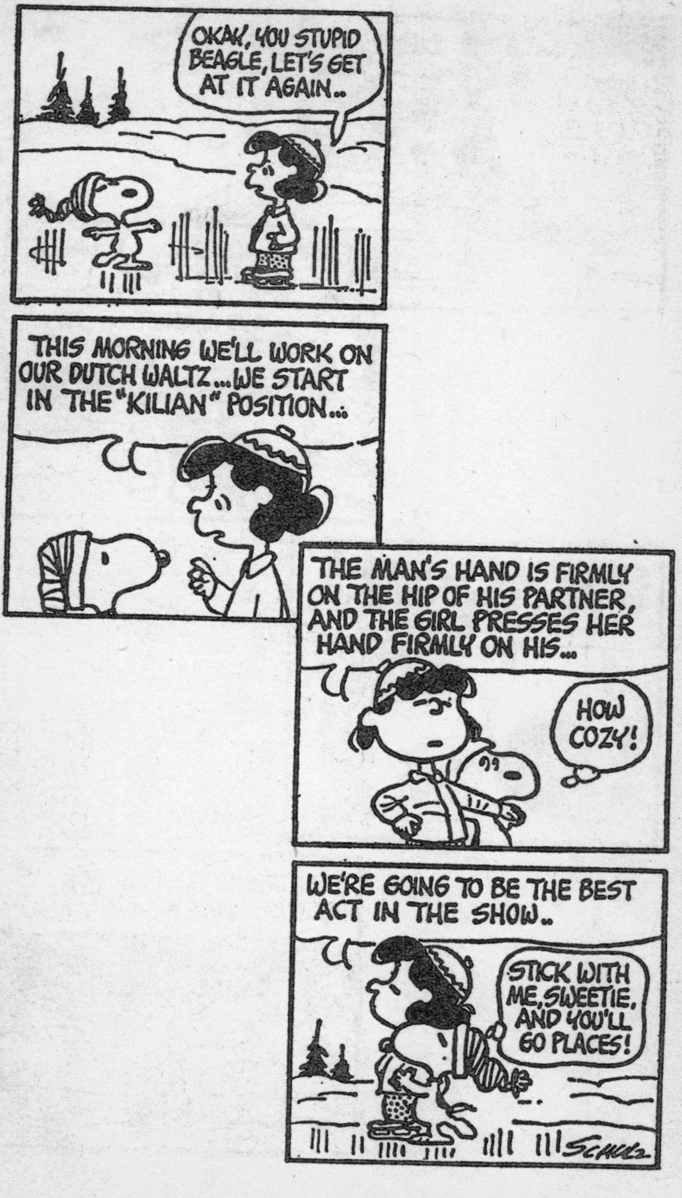
OKAY, YOU STUPID BEAGLE, LET'S GET AT IT AGAIN..
THIS MORNING WE'LL WORK ON OUR DUTCH WALTZ...WE START IN THE "KILIAN" POSITION...
THE MAN'S HAND IS FIRMLY ON THE HIP OF HIS PARTNER, AND THE GIRL PRESSES HER HAND FIRMLY ON HIS...
HOW COZY!
WE'RE GOING TO BE THE BEST ACT IN THE SHOW..
STICK WITH ME, SWEETIE, AND YOU'LL GO PLACES!
SCHULZ

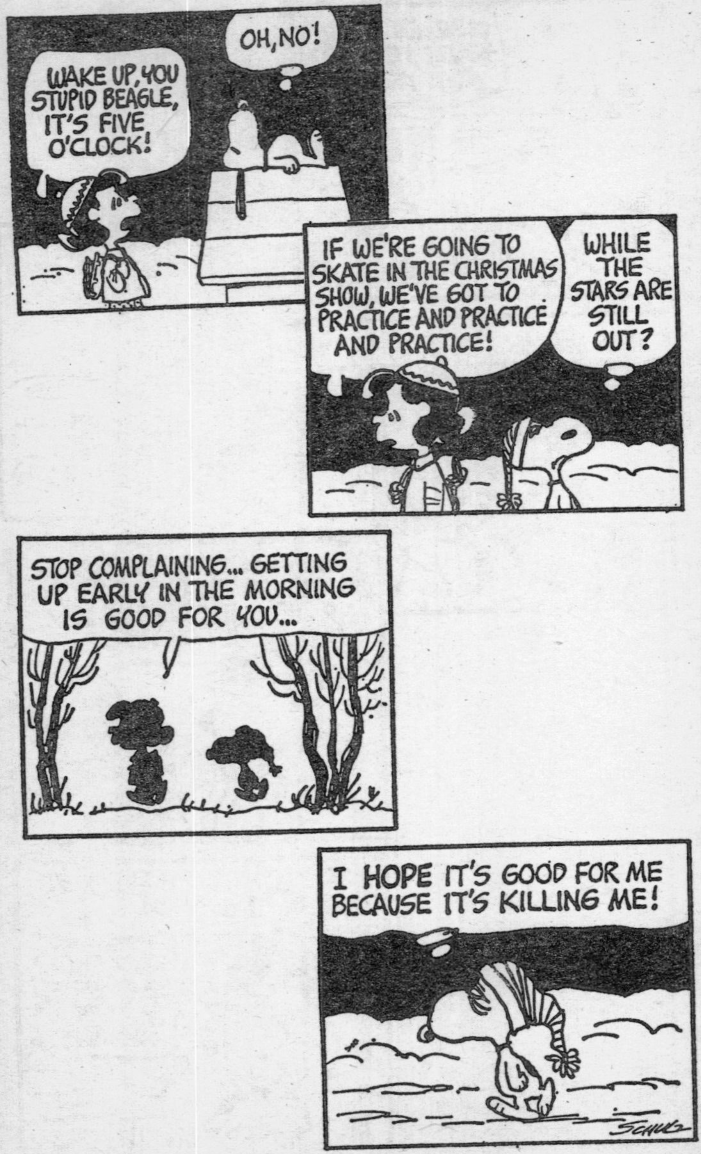
WAKE UP, YOU STUPID BEAGLE, IT'S FIVE O'CLOCK!
OH, NO!
IF WE'RE GOING TO SKATE IN THE CHRISTMAS SHOW, WE'VE GOT TO PRACTICE AND PRACTICE AND PRACTICE!
WHILE THE STARS ARE STILL OUT?
STOP COMPLAINING... GETTING UP EARLY IN THE MORNING IS GOOD FOR YOU...
I HOPE IT'S GOOD FOR ME BECAUSE IT'S KILLING ME!
SCHULZ

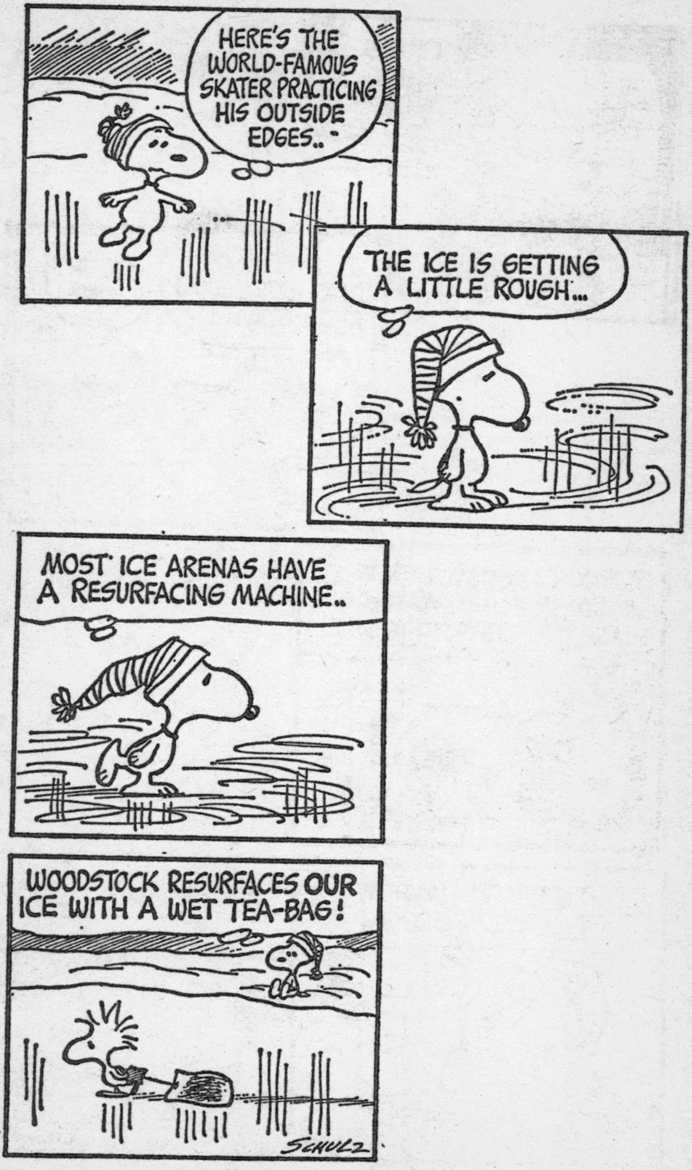
HERE'S THE WORLD-FAMOUS SKATER PRACTICING HIS OUTSIDE EDGES..
THE ICE IS GETTING A LITTLE ROUGH...
MOST ICE ARENAS HAVE A RESURFACING MACHINE..
WOODSTOCK RESURFACES OUR ICE WITH A WET TEA-BAG!
SCHULZ

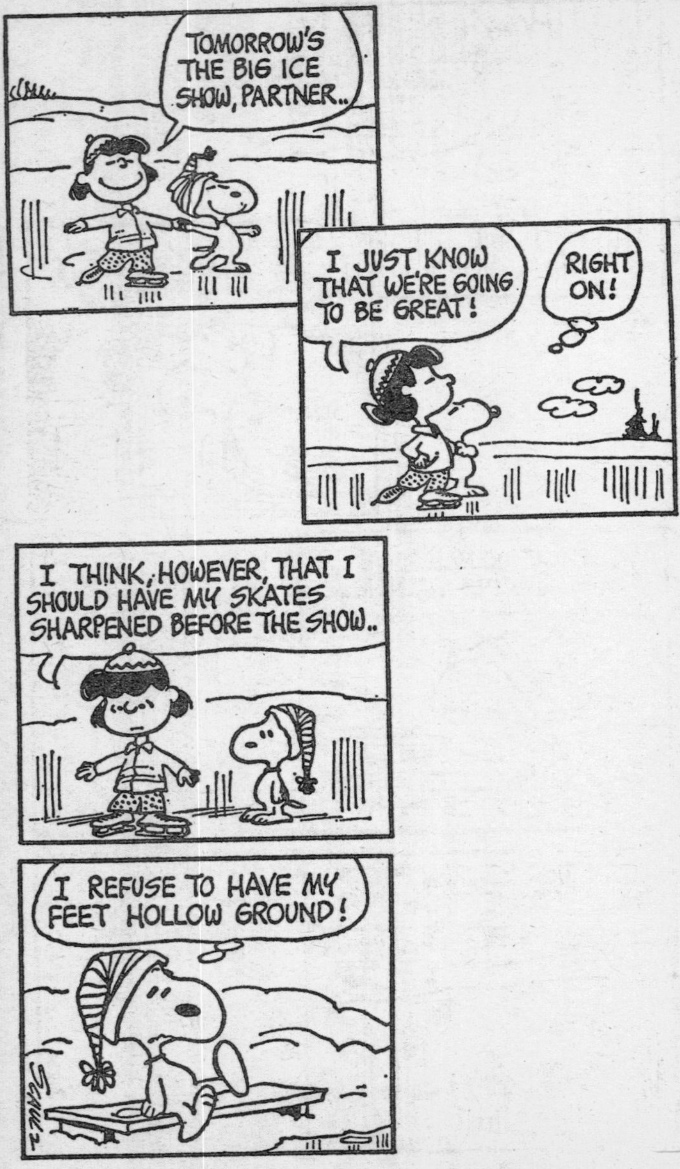
TOMORROW'S THE BIG ICE SHOW, PARTNER..
I JUST KNOW THAT WE'RE GOING TO BE GREAT!
RIGHT ON!
I THINK, HOWEVER, THAT I SHOULD HAVE MY SKATES SHARPENED BEFORE THE SHOW..
I REFUSE TO HAVE MY FEET HOLLOW GROUND!
SCHULZ

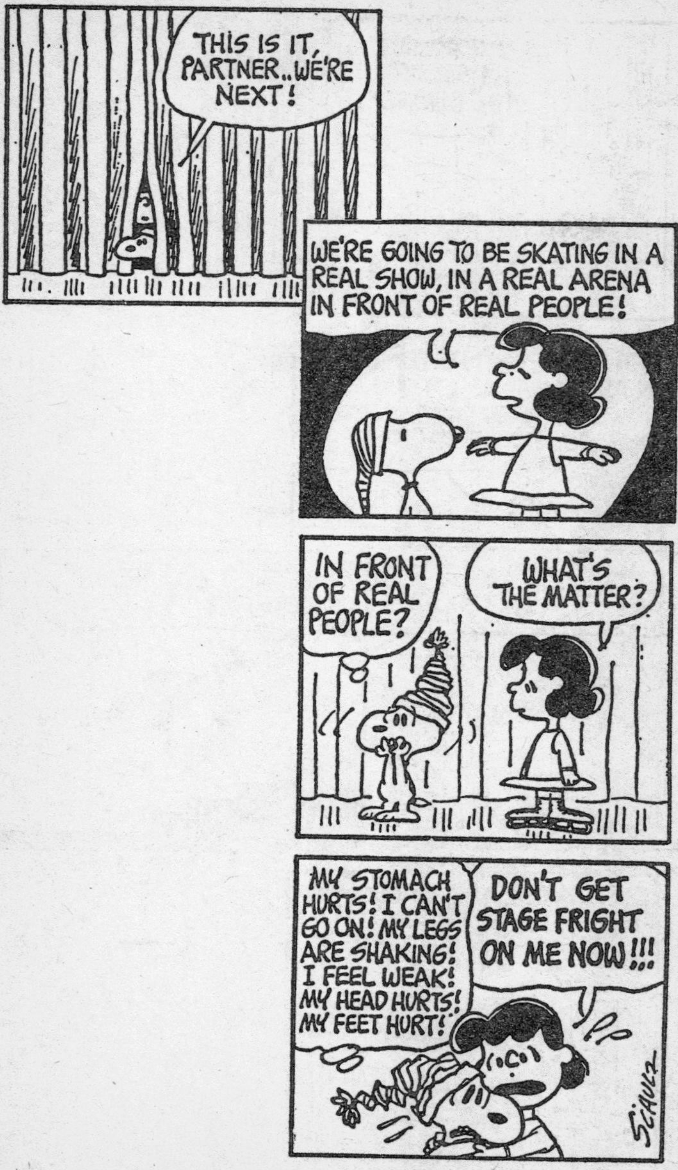
THIS IS IT, PARTNER..WE'RE NEXT!
WE'RE GOING TO BE SKATING IN A REAL SHOW, IN A REAL ARENA IN FRONT OF REAL PEOPLE!
IN FRONT OF REAL PEOPLE?
WHAT'S THE MATTER?
MY STOMACH HURTS! I CAN'T GO ON! MY LEGS ARE SHAKING! I FEEL WEAK! MY HEAD HURTS! MY FEET HURT!
DON'T GET STAGE FRIGHT ON ME NOW!!!
SCHULZ

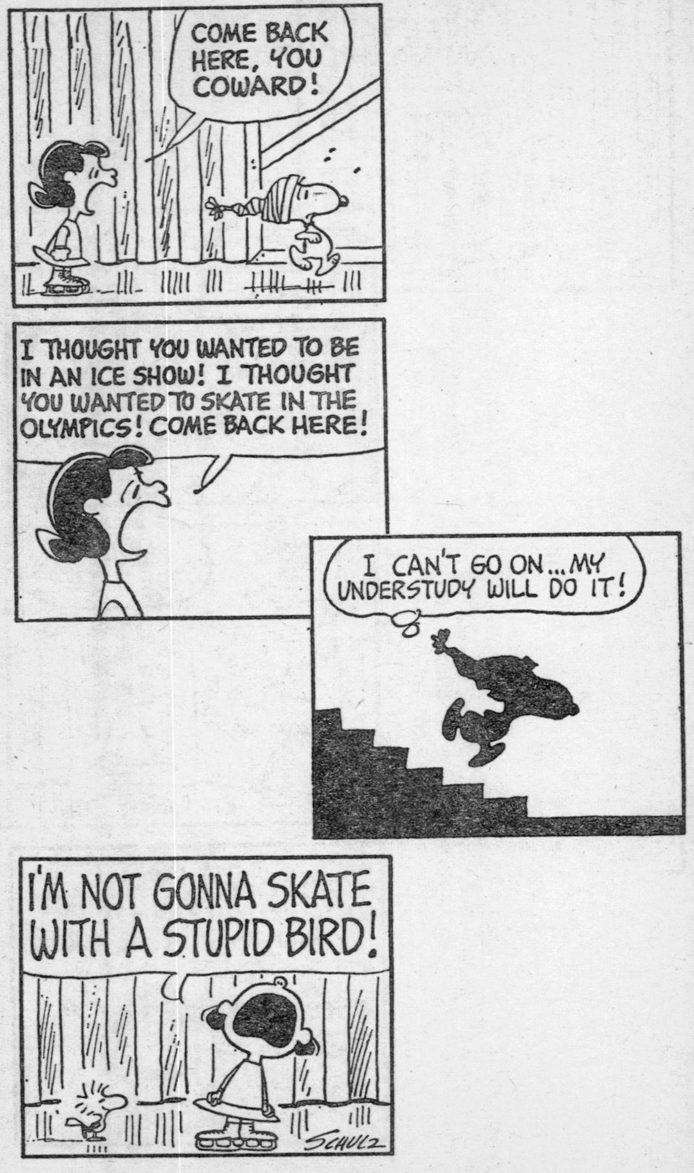
COME BACK HERE, YOU COWARD!
I THOUGHT YOU WANTED TO BE IN AN ICE SHOW! I THOUGHT YOU WANTED TO SKATE IN THE OLYMPICS! COME BACK HERE!
I CAN'T GO ON... MY UNDERSTUDY WILL DO IT!
I'M NOT GONNA SKATE WITH A STUPID BIRD!
SCHULZ

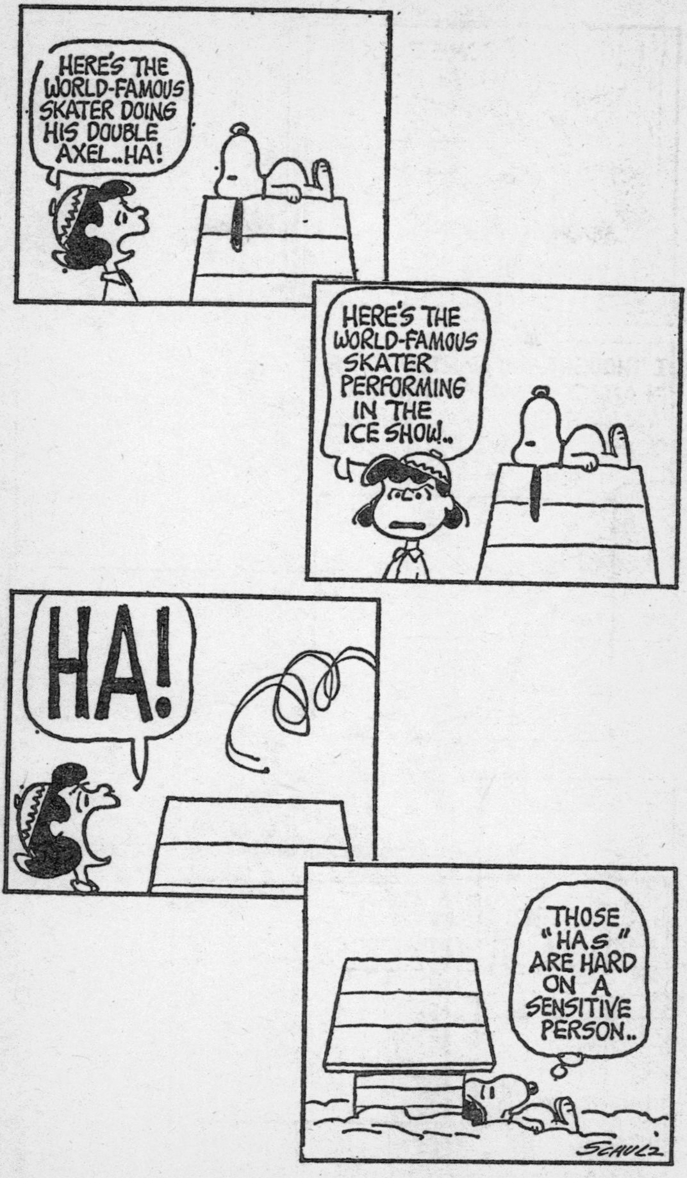
HERE'S THE WORLD-FAMOUS SKATER DOING HIS DOUBLE AXEL..HA!
HERE'S THE WORLD-FAMOUS SKATER PERFORMING IN THE ICE SHOW!..
HA!
THOSE "HAs" ARE HARD ON A SENSITIVE PERSON..
SCHULZ

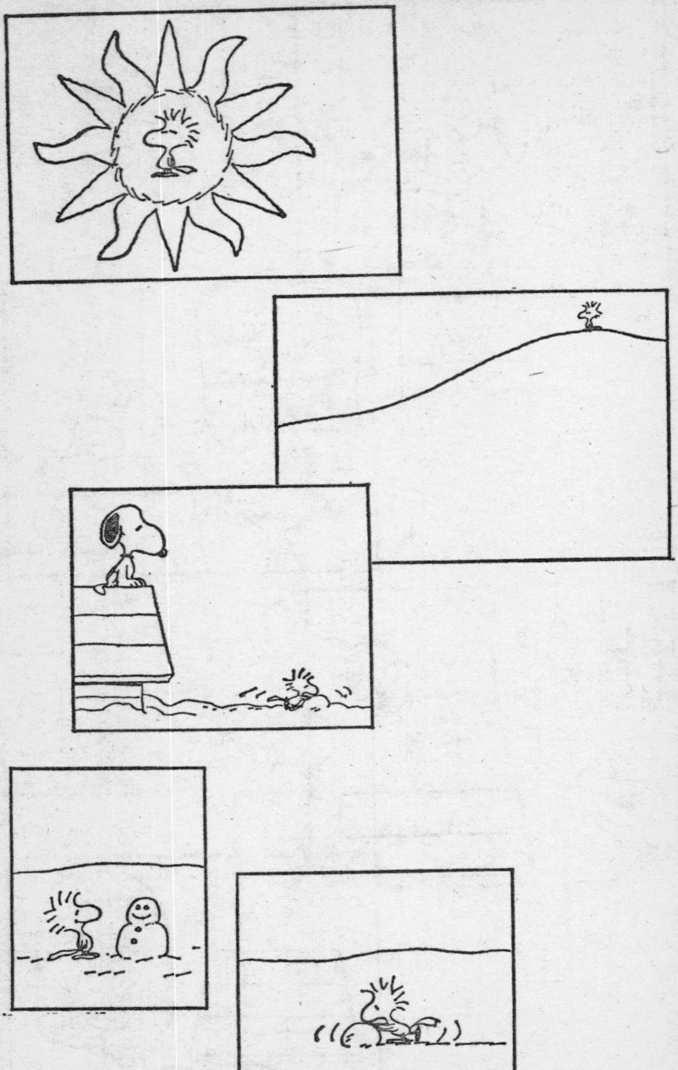

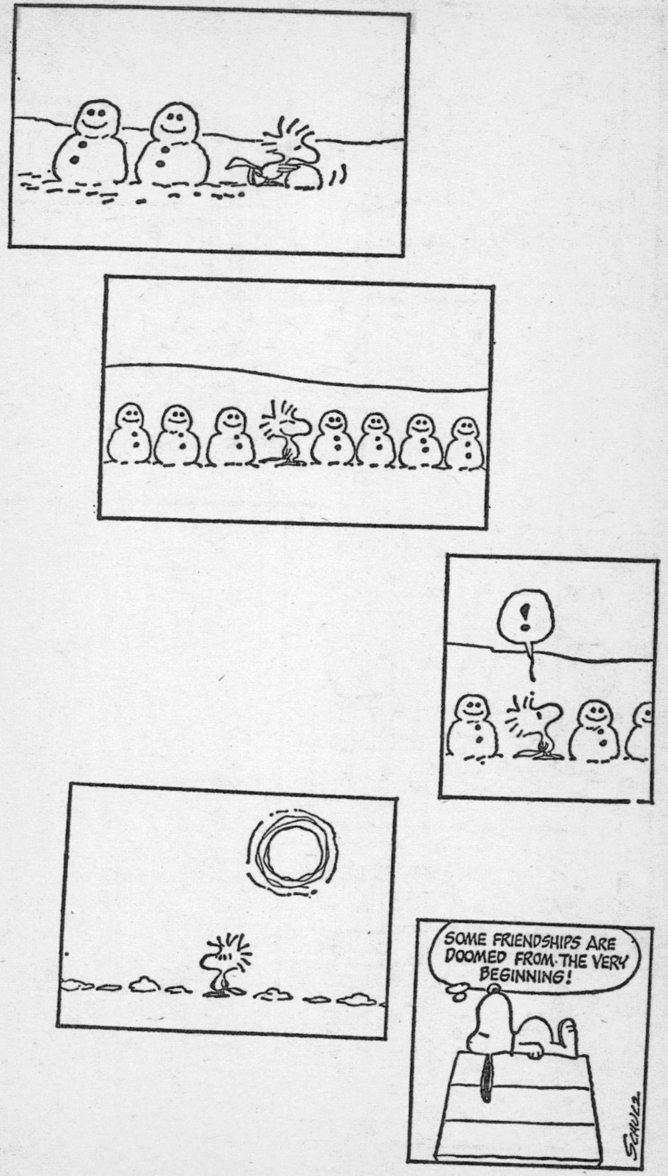
!
SOME FRIENDSHIPS ARE DOOMED FROM THE VERY BEGINNING!
SCHULZ

Z
Z
Z
THAT'S WHAT HAPPENS WHEN YOU HAVE NO ANXIETIES...
SCHULZ

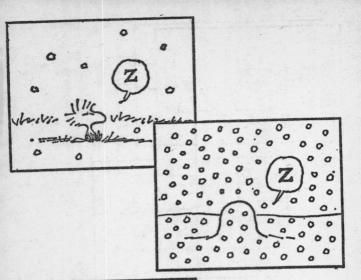

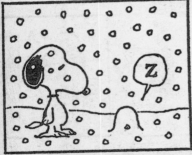

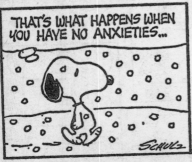

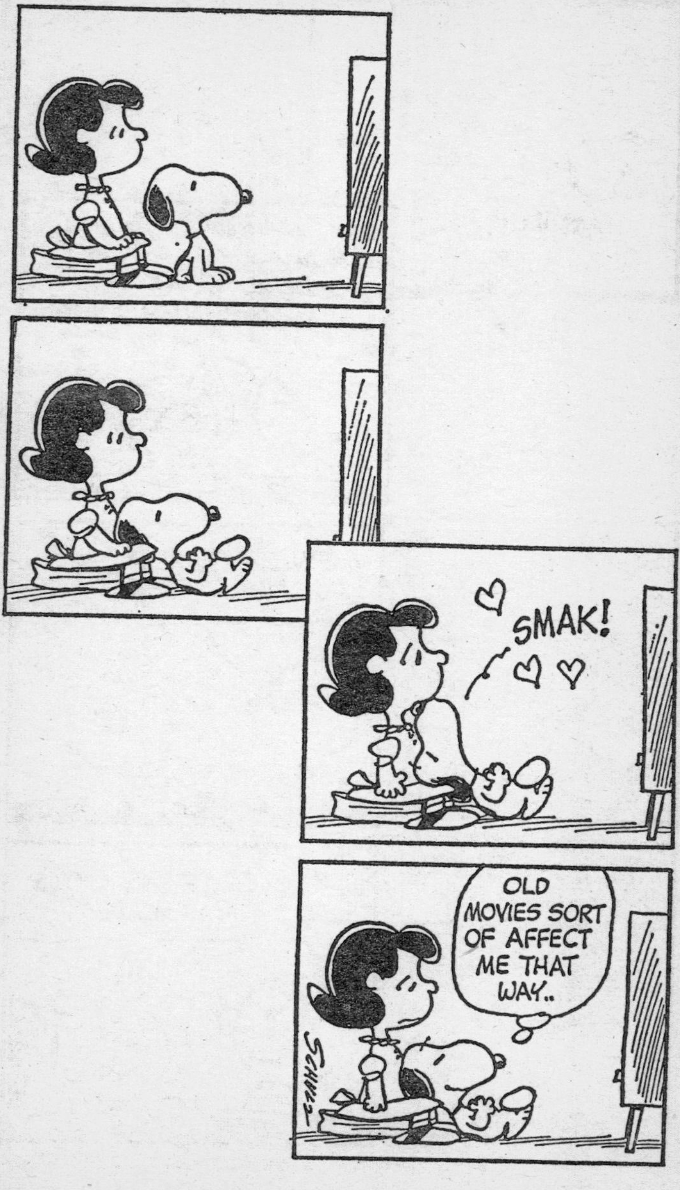
SMAK!
OLD MOVIES SORT OF AFFECT ME THAT WAY..
SCHULZ

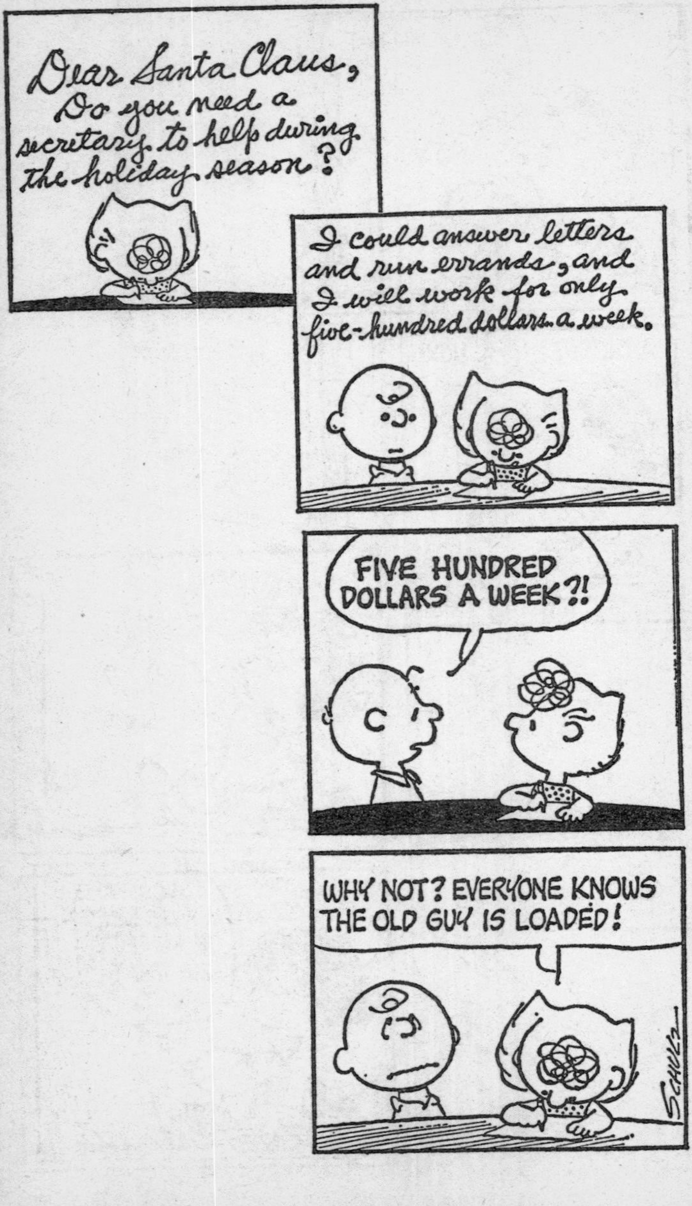
Dear Santa Claus,
Do you need a secretary to help during the holiday season?
I could answer letters and run errands, and I will work for only five-hundred dollars a week.
FIVE HUNDRED DOLLARS A WEEK?!
WHY NOT? EVERYONE KNOWS THE OLD GUY IS LOADED!
SCHULZ

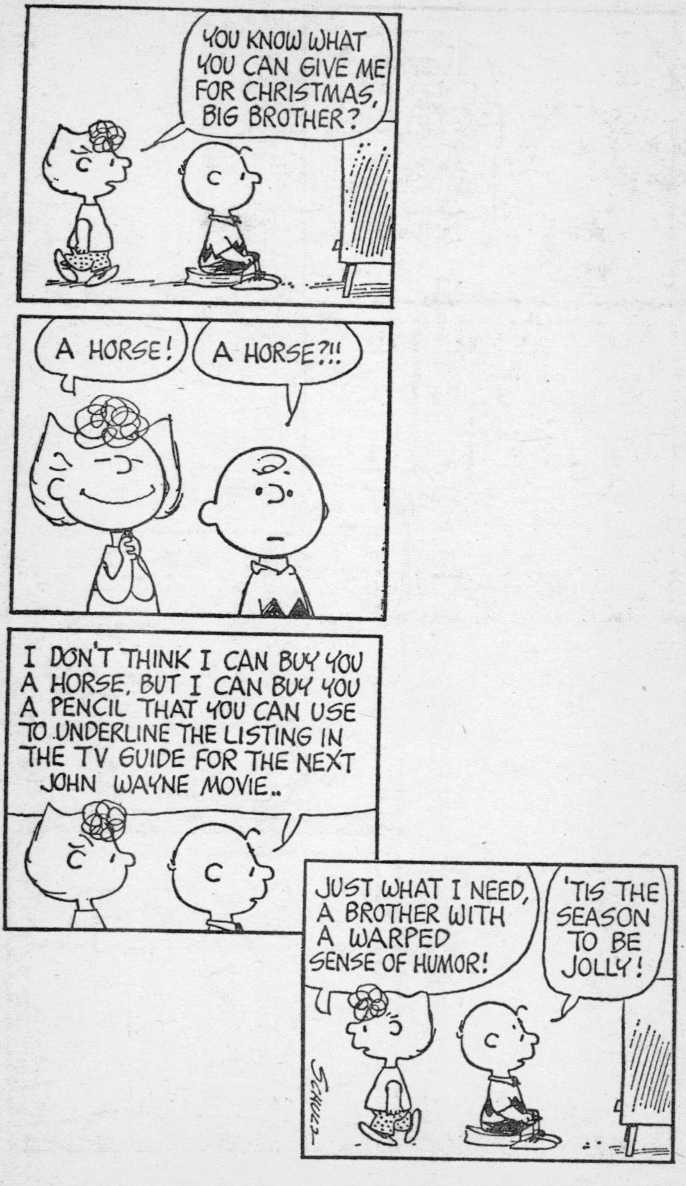
YOU KNOW WHAT YOU CAN GIVE ME FOR CHRISTMAS, BIG BROTHER?
A HORSE!
A HORSE?!!
I DON'T THINK I CAN BUY YOU A HORSE, BUT I CAN BUY YOU A PENCIL THAT YOU CAN USE TO UNDERLINE THE LISTING IN THE TV GUIDE FOR THE NEXT JOHN WAYNE MOVIE..
JUST WHAT I NEED, A BROTHER WITH A WARPED SENSE OF HUMOR!
'TIS THE SEASON TO BE JOLLY!
SCHULZ

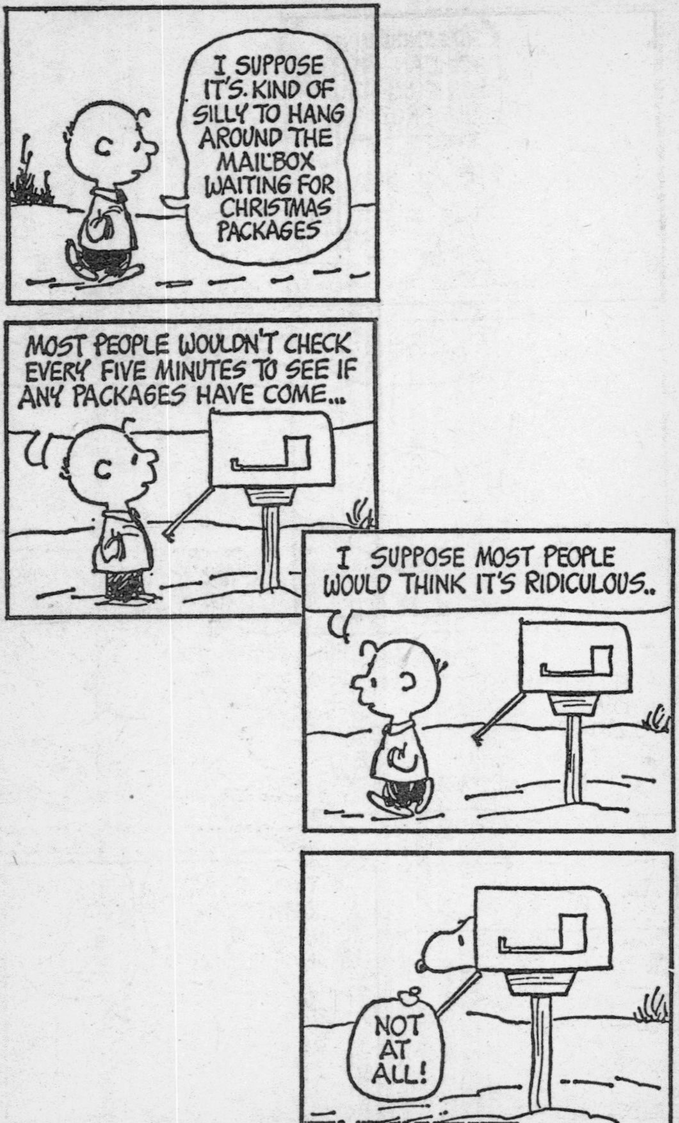
I SUPPOSE IT'S KIND OF SILLY TO HANG AROUND THE MAILBOX WAITING FOR CHRISTMAS PACKAGES
MOST PEOPLE WOULDN'T CHECK EVERY FIVE MINUTES TO SEE IF ANY PACKAGES HAVE COME...
I SUPPOSE MOST PEOPLE WOULD THINK IT'S RIDICULOUS..
NOT AT ALL!
SCHULZ

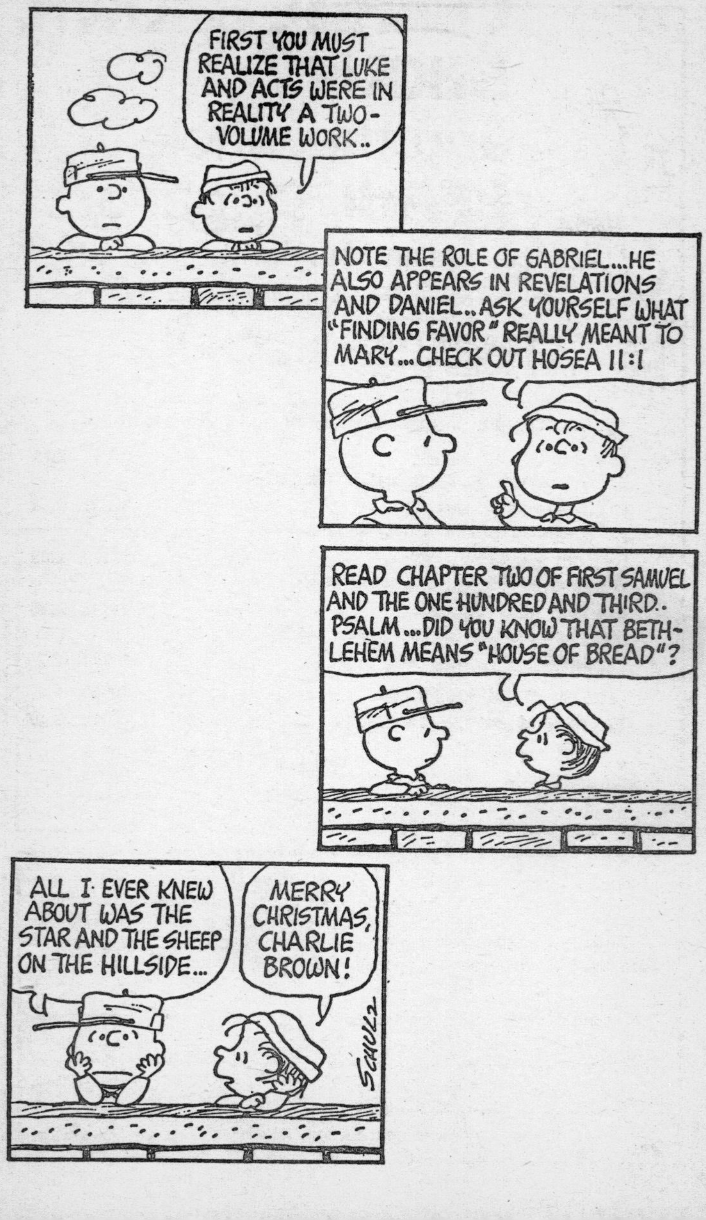
FIRST YOU MUST REALIZE THAT LUKE AND ACTS WERE IN REALITY A TWO-VOLUME WORK..
NOTE THE ROLE OF GABRIEL...HE ALSO APPEARS IN REVELATIONS AND DANIEL..ASK YOURSELF WHAT "FINDING FAVOR" REALLY MEANT TO MARY...CHECK OUT HOSEA 11:1
READ CHAPTER TWO OF FIRST SAMUEL AND THE ONE HUNDRED AND THIRD. PSALM...DID YOU KNOW THAT BETHLEHEM MEANS "HOUSE OF BREAD"?
ALL I EVER KNEW ABOUT WAS THE STAR AND THE SHEEP ON THE HILLSIDE...
MERRY CHRISTMAS, CHARLIE BROWN!
SCHULZ

Copr. © 1952
United Feature Syndicate, Inc.

CHARLIE BROWN, SNOOPY and the whole PEANUTS® gang...

together again with another set of daily trials and tribulations by

CHARLES M. SCHULZ

TAF-3